Theo Kemp is a New Zealand writer and musician of Anglo/Irish descent.

To all those people whose lives have been shattered by betrayal. Picking up the pieces and putting them back together again may be the hardest thing you ever do, but probably the most rewarding.

Theo Kemp

HEARTBREAK HOTEL DIARY

AUSTIN MACAULEY PUBLISHERS™

LONDON • CAMBRIDGE • NEW YORK • SHARJAH

A CIP catalogue record for this title is available from the British Library.

ISBN 9781398498471 (Paperback)
ISBN 9781398498488 (ePub e-book)

www.austinmacauley.com

First Published 2023
Austin Macauley Publishers Ltd®
1 Canada Square
Canary Wharf
London
E14 5AA

I would like to acknowledge my wonderful partner, who picked up the pieces and helped me put my life back together again. Without her kindness, care and non-judgmental support, this book would never have been written, and I probably wouldn't still be around.

Mostly written during the COVID-19 lockdowns, this is not a work of fiction, and represents a true representation of the author's thoughts and feelings during a difficult period in his life.

Table of Contents

I've Been Struggling

for a long time with the demons of betrayal and wondered if there is anyone out there going through similar problems. If you are, I'd like to share some of my experiences with you.

This is day one of my new Heartbreak Hotel Diary. For ages, I've been writing to myself, writing a diary of my feelings and mood changes trying to make some sort of sense of a senseless situation that sees me wallowing in the past and not moving on. Today, I thought, why not share these experiences with others in the hope that what I'm feeling, you are feeling. A problem shared is a problem halved, so they say.

Sometimes I feel that other people just don't understand. They tell me how they coped with a breakup in the past and that it's just a matter of time. But usually, it was one of many relationship failures that seem to be a part of growing up. Mine was different, over 24 years of a committed relationship that was the first for me. One I never thought would end, no matter how many hurdles we needed to jump. But end it did in the most heartbreaking of ways for me. Lies, adultery and humiliation. What a way to treat another human being who loved and supported in such a completely selfless way. Maybe I'm too sensitive, maybe I'll never get over the betrayal?

But these diary entries mustn't be about self-pity, they must be about finding a way out of the frequent lows. They should be about finding techniques that allow us to move forward with our lives and leave the pain behind. Writing these entries has been cathartic for me and I hope that what I have to say will be cathartic for you. Please join me on my journey of self-discovery, I think we will learn a lot together.

Blocking out Negative Thoughts

If only I could discover a bit more about myself and learn how to deal with the internal turmoil that seems to pervade my mind for most of the time. Constant unhelpful thoughts from the past run around my brain spoiling the present and confusing the future. There must be a way through this and I'm determined to find the route, not only for me but for all the other unfortunate people that have to put up with this nonsense. I've read lots of self-help books during the course of my life and deep down, they have probably taught me a lot. But you know what? It's all very well reading the books, but you won't get anywhere until you start putting the recommendations into action. Besides, sometimes I get self-help overload and I'm jammed so full of touchy-feely, positive-thinking, every-thing-is-possible vibes, I just freeze up. It's a by-product of positive-thinking overload.

Talking of books, I read a great one recently called *Make Brilliant Work*. Rod Judkins is a British artist who trained at the Royal College of Art. His ideas are succinct and pithy. I like that and should try to emulate his writing style. He weaves stories about real people—usually famous—into his text to emphasize a point and uses their failures and subsequent successes as a source of inspiration. On the whole, it works. Many of his arguments revolve around bucking the system in order to come up with something truly original. Conformity leads to conformity and accepting the status quo produces nothing more than the status quo. It's a very relevant point in this age of sameness. We need to find a way to break the mould and look at everything with fresh eyes and ears.

However, there must be a trick to doing this without rocking the boat too much. The famous classical composer Mozart managed to do this by writing music that pleased the powers-that-be, but also challenged the accepted forms and harmonic structures of the time. His contemporary Haydn was even more subversive, managing to get away with brilliantly quirky compositions that probably left many of his contemporary commentators scratching their heads.

Beethoven, of course, didn't give a damn about rocking the boat, he mostly pulled the whole thing over!

Our challenge then might be to find a soft enough approach that allows things to change without ruffling too many feathers. But this goes against the grain for me because I'm naturally a feather ruffler and don't like conformity in any shape or form. A lot of this spirit comes from my father who rejected society, left his job and took all of us from a comfortable house in the South of England to live in a two-up, two-down terraced house in Yorkshire. He then took my brother and me out of the system and home-schooled us. It was a brave move and one my brother thinks came out of a nervous breakdown. I'm not so sure, although I think my father's mental state was a trifle precarious at times and there seems to be quite a bit of this in the family. But that's another story and one I might share at another time.

The instability of the mind might be part of my own problem and one that exacerbates negative thought processes. But where is the dividing line between stability and instability? I've only been to two sessions with a counsellor in my whole life. The first didn't really help as he spent most of the time filling out forms and then advised me to cheat on my wife if she was cheating on me. Hardly a constructive suggestion when you are suffering immense pain from being betrayed. The second, more recent session, was with a lovely guy who was very reassuring but obviously didn't think there was too much wrong with me. Maybe I have sorted things out in my mind on the surface, but there is still a hell of a lot bubbling away underneath.

It's all down to the neural pathways in our mind and how we keep re-treading our steps mentally, over and over again. If you go for a walk on the North Yorkshire Moors (where I grew up), you see the sheep tracks through the bracken and heather, made by sheep taking the same route for years and years. We do that with our negative thinking, constantly going through the same negative thought patterns over and over again. Over and over again. Over and over again. Get the message? In a failed relationship, we start to relive the good times and regret their passing. We start to blame ourselves for not making enough effort to keep the relationship alive. We go through the 'if only I'd done more' or 'if only I'd been more attentive' or 'if only I'd seen the writing on the wall.' But this is ridiculous because we are forgetting about the psychological bullying and the eggshell walking that led to that point. We forget about the anger and the ultimate betrayal. We even forget about the years of subsequent mental anguish we've suffered and how washed out it's left us. We forget about the feelings of total abandonment and being lost in the world—a rudderless ship just drifting in a vast ocean of nothingness. We forget about how understanding we tried to be and how devoted we were to the relationship. Well, maybe we shouldn't forget.

When the rose-tinted neural pathways start appearing in our minds and those pervasive synapses start clicking, we must stop the rot there and then, long before the waves of pain and regret take hold of us. We deserve better than a life of waking up to that kind of internal torture. I've been through that agony for two and a half years and it's the cruellest experience I've ever had. However, breaking the habit is easier said than done as you and I know. I think I've tried every technique in the book. After the first months of sheer panic and nightly sweats accompanied by very little sleep—I just didn't want to fall asleep because I'd wake up to the same nightmare—I found a distraction and tried to concentrate my mind on that one thing to blot out every other thought. I've continued to try and use this method with varying degrees of success for a long time. But blotting out the negative thoughts by whatever means may be the only way.

Resentment

Well, here we are again. It's a later start this morning because I drank too much wine last night and had a throbbing head for most of the night. Drinking too much is such a silly thing to do, but a difficult habit to break. At the time it seems such a good idea and the blurred edges it creates are very addictive. It's escapism of course and designed to take our mind off the here and now and any possible unsolved problems we might have. Having said that, it can be quite inspiring and help to get the creative juices going. It's good for brainstorming sessions and helps the ideas flow. I read recently that Michelangelo spent more on wine than he did on marble and the ancient philosophers certainly got through a fair amount of therapy bottles/jugs.

But overall, overindulgence probably isn't the best idea, particularly, if it takes a day or so to get over the resultant hangover. In the last couple of years, I've demolished an enormous amount of therapy bottles. I think the tide is gradually turning on my drinking habits as the headaches remind me of my decreasing drinking stamina. Probably a good thing too. So that's the drinking story of the day.

During my two-hour walk yesterday, I thought about all manner of things. I was a bit grumpy to start with because my lovely partner didn't want to join me for the first part of my walk. I felt that we could be losing our sense of connection as I so enjoyed our walks together in the past. It can be dangerous to become dependent on the people around you to lift your spirits and provide a constant support service. It's a bit selfish to expect them to pander to your every whim. Even in the closest of relationships, we all need our personal space and it's important that we grow individually as much as together. I love doing everything with my new partner, but I'm also aware that in the past, such a close bond led to its own set of problems. I was so devoted to my previous relationship, I forgot who I was and felt that my only role in life was to support my wife. Unfortunately, after time, that kind of devotion made me overdependent and unattractive. I lost any sense of self-worth in the process of trying to build her up. I did everything in my power to make her strong and independent and it worked. She became so strong and independent, she didn't need me! I became unnecessary baggage that was all too easily trashed after over 20 years together. So no, we shouldn't become too dependent on our partners or our friends.

We need to build our own internal strength in the first instance because that is the only thing that will get us through what life sometimes throws at us. We never know what's around the corner, what's over the hill or even what's going to bite us on the bum from the most unlikely source. I think the phrase 'mental health' is probably a good one. If we have a strong sense of who we are and an internal conviction that we are happy with ourselves, we can survive the cruel salvos, no matter what they may be.

Coming from this position of personal strength, we can also decide what is important to us, rather than what is important to those around us. This isn't necessarily a selfish attitude since suppressing our own desires and wishes in order to keep other people happy leads to resentment. No relationship will work with any form of resentment present. The trick is to come to an understanding that is based on mutual agreement, not self-sacrifice. Both partners retain their own personal integrity but also understand that there will always need to be things that are negotiated. In my own case, I need to understand that my partner feels the need to run rather than walk, at least for some of the way. She feels the need to raise her pulse rate in order to feel physically satisfied. I need to understand and accept that and not read any other meaning into it, like rejection or abandonment or any other of those self-deprecating emotions that the mind can create.

When resentment pervades a relationship, negative thoughts run riot. Both parties start to rot from within, engulfed by an internal disease that eats away at everything they hold dear. It's like an imploding black hole that can't be saved. Inevitably, one or other of the couple will be so consumed by the inequality, they will get their ultimate revenge and betray the relationship, no matter how long it has survived. It is a heartbreaking scenario and one that could probably be avoided with some positive and constructive steps. But the lines of communication breakdown. Neither party is willing to accept any form of responsibility or find some middle ground to work things out. Instead, the resentment becomes buried and ultimately one of the pair plots an escape route subversively. They have an affair and break the trust that has been in place for a very long time. It's a very sad end to something beautiful and leaves permanent scars on both people. Maybe both their lives will be better in the long run, but who knows?

We must learn from our experiences and make sure we don't make the same mistakes again. The emotional scars will stay with us forever, but they mustn't ruin the rest of our lives. Everything we do in life is a learning experience, both good and bad. If we are irreparably damaged by every event, we won't last very long.

Victimhood

I thought a lot about writing thoughts down after I got into bed last night. I thought about how therapeutic it can be mentally. I thought about how writing has helped me get through some of the challenges life has thrown at me. I think it is a good way to organise the mind and release some of the pent-up tension that inevitably accrues during the course of our daily lives. It's a kind of mental escape valve for us all.

I've been tempted to give up on life. But I know it's an attitude of mind and a tendency on my part to assume the role of an emotional victim. Life has thrown all of these things at me, so how can I possibly cope? I am the poor innocent person who has had to endure so much. It's an easy position to inhabit, but a very dangerous one too. Anyone can be an emotional victim if they allow themselves to be one. In most circumstances, it is something we decide to become. Of course, if another person fires a gun at us, or attacks us with a knife, we may unwittingly become a victim, but that's something quite different and has nothing to do with emotional victimhood.

My father was a writer and a very talented one too. But his style was more technical than mine. He wrote articles about printing and business and less about the states of the mind. Having said that, his letters to me whilst I was at college were full of sound advice and couched in very encouraging terms. He was a very good man, but he also had his problems—as we all do. In the end, he couldn't cope with society and withdrew into his own world. My mother was a good woman and devoted to him, so went along with it all. But his own world was often inhabited by demons that pushed him to the edge of sanity. He believed that he was always at the mercy of 'the fathers of daughters.' He had three sons of course, so I guess, that was his justification! Truth be told, he was a classic case of victimhood.

By writing things down, I think I have just learnt something about myself. I think we are all influenced by our parents and often those influences become buried. Either we don't want to admit it or convince ourselves we are completely different people and can't possibly fall into the same traps that they fell into. We are the new 'improved' versions of our parents. It's a nice theory, but probably for the most part erroneous.

Another facet of victimhood is to blame. We blame the other people in our lives for not helping us, or even for deliberately holding us back. It's another destructive scenario that can ruin our lives and push the people closest to us away. If we are a victim, everything that happens in our lives must be someone else's fault. If we are overweight, we blame our genetics; if we don't progress in our careers, we blame our upbringing or our teachers or our boss. It's a ludicrous position to take and one that drains us of any sense of responsibility. However many advantages we have had and opportunities we have been given, just don't register on our victimhood psyche.

Positive Images for a Positive Way Ahead

Good morning, world! I'm feeling a bit more upbeat today after an excellent sleep. It's amazing how these mood swings go up and down. When the shit hit the fan two and a half years ago, my sleep patterns were completely turned upside down. Difficult getting to sleep and then waking up in the middle of the night mulling over every aspect of my life. Mainly blaming myself for what happened, even when it wasn't sensible to take responsibility for everything. Most of all, it was trying to come to terms with the betrayal and break of trust; that, and the lies and deception. That is something I don't think I'll ever really come to terms with. How can anyone do that to another human being, let alone someone they supposedly loved for such a long time? It's beyond me because I couldn't.

Having said that, when I'm having a good day like today, I can be a little more pragmatic and forget about the hideous few years I've been through. When I'm feeling strong, there is an inner conviction that I'm actually better off without this person in my life. Perhaps, they did us both a favour and their bravery should be celebrated not condemned. But to be honest, those feelings don't last very long. If someone wants to escape from a relationship, they should be open and honest and not treat the other person with contempt. In the end, so openly lying and creating all manner of fictions to cover their tracks. Furthermore, sniggering with their newfound love and spitting on their past. Truly distasteful and contemptible.

If only these good days would last. If this inner strength would carry on for more than a few weeks at a time. Sadly, there's been a pattern of ups and downs for me lasting the whole two and a half years. Admittedly, the downs were a daily occurrence for the first year and a half and then gradually became more spread out. But it still takes only the smallest of triggers to set another one in motion. I had one of those a few weeks back with friends telling me something about my ex that I really didn't want to know. Despite telling them I didn't want to know anything at all about her, they still couldn't help themselves. It sent me back into another downward spiral, going over the whole sordid episode over and over again. Questioning myself and how I had reacted, never remembering the hurt and despicable way I was treated, just remembering the good times and how I miss them. Back to waking up every morning with a sick feeling in my stomach and a sense of worthlessness. Back to feeling trapped in a pointless existence that I can't possibly escape from. Back to feeling I will never have a life so good ever again. Back to beating myself up for screwing things up.

When we are at a low ebb, these feelings are all-consuming and pervasive and there seems to be little we can do to escape. But it is very important to try and break the cycle by remembering the stress and the eggshell walking, the bullying and the cruelty. Deliberately discard thoughts that would lead onto that ever-so-painful treadmill of regret and longing for the good times from the past. At some stage, we may be able to look back on those times objectively and appreciate they were a good part of our lives, but whilst we are still vulnerable that just isn't possible. We must protect ourselves with thoughts of now and how better off we are to be out of such a toxic relationship and be away from a liar and a cheat. We must also be firm about not taking the blame for the situation that arose.

I find it useful to have an image in my mind that I can refer to when the negative, self-deprecating thoughts start to materialise. At the moment, I have a dream house in mind, one set in its own grounds and filled with trees and the resultant bird life. I've found an image for one that's for sale on the internet. My mind is full of internal and external pictures of it and I can switch to these whenever I want to. I've used these distracting devices in the past too. In the early days, I had quotes placed above the toilet so whenever I went for a pee, I repeated them to myself. One was 'You are not what happened to you, you are what you choose to become.' There were many like that and they really did help. But now I think something visual is more effective, particularly when you first wake up and your mind tends to go to well-trodden neural pathways. However, it doesn't need to be a house, of course, it could be any picture that fills you with hope and optimism for the future.

Letting Go

Last night, I dreamt about my ex yet again. These days, the dreams aren't so abandonment-focused, which is a great relief. They do, however, have undercurrents of criticism. I'm always feeling that I've done something wrong, that somehow any situation that arises in the dream is my fault. Ludicrous or what? I think these sorts of internal scars take some time to heal. Even if I've managed to switch off the conscious internal babble about her, the subconscious mind is still doing the processing.

When do we finally let go, that's the big question. Do we ever let go? I certainly hope so, because I don't want to be haunted by this cruel woman for the rest of my life. Someone who broke my heart a million times over and spat on our relationship. I guess most normal people let go a lot quicker than me. I shouldn't be dreaming about my ex after two and a half years; I should be concentrating on my new relationship with an amazing woman who doesn't manipulate me in any of the nasty ways my ex did. So, what's holding me back? I guess it's over twenty years of programming. I became accustomed to reacting in a certain way and it's difficult to change the habit.

When I first met my new partner, she told me I was always checking her face for approval. I'd say something and look at her to make sure I was saying the right thing. This was an ingrained reaction and I wasn't even aware of it. Of course, we always want to please the one we love and don't want to say anything that might upset them, but this sort of confirmation had become extreme. It came out of the constant criticism I was subjected to. Towards the end of my marriage, I knew that whatever I suggested would be rubbished. Every comment I made would be ridiculed or at the very least, double-checked. I was treated with contempt and disdain. If someone else suggested the very same thing, that would be fine, but what I had to say was worthless. I guess it is the classic example of being henpecked. When it first started, I stood up for myself and questioned her approach, but the more I unravelled her argument and often exposed it as fallacious, the more extreme her stance became. She would start to focus on something that had nothing whatsoever to do with the topic and become very angry. After a while, I realised the best thing to do to avoid an argument was to agree with her. With every rebuttal, I would simply take a deep breath and smile sweetly.

Unfortunately, the by-product of constant criticism is that you begin to close up and retreat into your own shell, just for self-protection. You bottle things up and are afraid to air your concerns for fear of a backlash. It's hard to even like someone who treats you with contempt. The deep-down love is always there—and that is something I always maintained—but it was difficult to feel the warmth that used to be there. I know this is all sounding very one-sided and that is really unfair, but I'm merely trying to explain how situations arise and how things can get out of hand. There were obviously many extenuating circumstances for my ex and I'd be foolish not to accept that. However, we need to feel respected in order to feel warmth towards another person. When that respect goes, so does the warmth. Towards the end, my ex often accused me of not showing her enough affection and of bottling things up. Well, as we've seen, the reasons for that were obvious.

I think I became scared of my former wife. She controlled almost every part of my life and made all the decisions. With hindsight, I let it all happen because it was the easiest thing to do. Her mother was a control freak and I guess the older my ex got, the more like her mother she became. Once again—and I've talked about this in a previous entry—it's hard to avoid parental influence. One bully morphs into another.

As I've said in the past, it's important to retain a certain amount of independence in any relationship and certainly work on loving *yourself*. Not in any narcissistic way, but to avoid becoming completely subsumed by someone else.

Keep Communicating

Predictably, I don't really know what I'm going to write about this morning. I usually start and a theme emerges. It probably isn't the most effective way to communicate, but it works for me. As I've said previously, most of what I do here is cathartic and designed to declutter my mind at the start of the day. Fortunately, since I began this diary, my spirits have been fairly up rather than down. I'm not sure if my daily musings have had an influence on this or if it's simply one of those 'up' periods. I guess I'll know when the next downer hits!

I did question myself yesterday after finishing 'Letting Go.' It seemed to me that by writing all that stuff, I was hardly letting go! But I reconciled myself with the thought that letting go comes in all sorts of shapes and forms. Some people let go by never thinking about what has happened and burying it. Others prefer a stealthy approach, extracting things gradually from the subconscious mind and dealing with them one by one. I think I'm the latter type. A good friend advised me to do this in the very early stages of my relationship nightmare. I don't know the Harry Potter stories well, but he likened it to a character swirling thoughts around in a cauldron and being able to pick individual ones out to deal with separately. I like that image. Perhaps the downers come along when we become swamped by a mass of unhelpful thoughts. We get engulfed by negativity and hamstrung by our own thoughts. Maybe my daily diary helps me to concentrate on one idea at a time and think through it.

I do think it is important to have some form of focus when dealing with a traumatic event in our lives, be it the end of an important relationship which is a form of grief, grief itself, when someone close to us dies, or any number of other curve balls that come our way. For some, it's work and the need to make a living. I was so devastated, I just couldn't cope with work. I just couldn't concentrate on what I needed to do. I forced myself in the initial stages, but in the end, I had to run away and find a supportive place to rest and lick my wounds. During that period of time, I joined every dating site I could find. It was a completely alien environment for me and one that I really wasn't suited to. Rather than writing quick messages to appropriate matches, I wrote mini novels. Needless to say, I was hopeless and only managed two dates in two months, despite making the process my number one priority. I always thought that honesty was what everyone wanted, so even my profile was from the heart. I soon discovered there is a lot of superficiality out there and it's quite difficult to connect with genuine people. But just when I was about to give up, I hit the jackpot and met my new partner. It was a new site for me and she was one of the first set of matches. We share the same profession and interests so that probably helped enormously.

I think that the moral of the story is to keep communicating with other people during a crisis. Realise that the world is a big place and there are people out there going through exactly what we are going through. Of course, there is superficiality and often the dating game is just that, a game. But eventually, if we persevere, we can all hit the jackpot. I'm not suggesting dating sites are always the answer, but the good ones certainly help the process on its way. There isn't the same sort of stigma associated with such things these days either, which is a real step forward. Whatever way we choose, we must find people who can help make us realise there is still a life after the one we have left behind. It's difficult to understand at the time, despite what friends may be telling us (and mutual friends is a difficult subject in itself), but it's true. However, ultimately, we can only find solutions to our own problems ourselves.

Mutual Friends and Support Networks

Yesterday, I mentioned the role mutual friends take on in a relationship breakup and how difficult it can be to manage the situation. After experiencing first-hand your heartbreak when your partner left you, they often change sides and start to feed comments that almost certainly come straight from your ex. It's a painful experience and one that's difficult to understand. To be sure, they are simply trying to see both sides of the situation and treat both parties fairly. But inevitably it can lead to a 'he said this,' 'she said that' situation that only keeps the pain alive. From their point of view, it isn't pain, of course, just a gathering of information to supposedly make an informed decision.

I decided to break the cycle and refused to counterpunch. I wasn't interested in getting into any to-and-fro exchanges with mutual friends in the middle. As a result, I lost most of them. However, ultimately, it's their choice. If they can't understand it can be painful hearing about the person who betrayed you, they really don't deserve to be friends anyway. If they don't have the sensitivity to tread very carefully and only want to apportion blame, we are better off without them.

In my situation, the strangest thing happened. When my wife left me for her new man (after months of deception and lies), I needed my friends and went to see them to explain honestly what had happened. I was devastated and it was plain to see my heartbreak. They seemed to be very understanding and supportive. Not long afterwards, I began to get the distinct impression the tide had turned and now everything was my fault. It's quite upsetting that suddenly the loyal devoted partner is at fault and the liar and cheat is the injured party. Quite bizarre really. Unfortunately, the manipulation carries on as do the lies. Sadly, in order to avoid everything dragging on endlessly with continued pain, you need to break loose from the cycle and stop it. Mutual friends become collateral damage in the breakup. If they are true friends, they will still keep in touch, even if it is just occasional contact. Having witnessed first-hand how upset you were, they should know better. They should also know better because they know you were a loyal, supportive and devoted partner for a very long time. But they are wooed by the ex and her now unchallenged webs of deception. Such is life and we must learn to live with it.

Of course, there are always two sides to a story and mine is only one of them. Maybe if my ex had the opportunity to explain herself, you would side with the ex-mutual friends. Who knows? There might be many valid reasons for my wife leaving me, but there is no valid reason for being a bully, a liar and a cheat. There is no valid reason for humiliating someone who always loved and supported you. The process needs to be better. Is it really necessary to be so cruel? I don't think so and it doesn't bode well for any future relationship on their part.

The classic cases of adultery and betrayal nearly always involve a man, so my case was less typical. In a way, the standard roles were reversed. In an age when more and more women are becoming independent and forging careers of their own (quite rightly so), they have the option to opt-out, cut loose and start over again. However, when they do the dirty, it just doesn't seem to come with the same fallout that their male equivalents attract. If a man cheats on his wife, he is considered a rat and a heartless scoundrel. If a woman does the same thing and dumps her loyal and devoted husband, she must have had good reasons and she obviously deserved something better. The support networks are always there for women because for generations, the 'homemaker' was traditionally a woman and it was a woman who needed propping up after her philandering husband betrayed her. It's interesting that the very word 'philandering' refers to men, not women, so ingrained are our prejudices (even though the original word had quite the opposite meaning). Any female equivalent, like a harlot or jezebel, seldom sees the light of day.

Without support networks in place for men, they often flounder and find themselves in a terribly lonely place. Generally speaking, we are not very good at discussing our feelings with anyone, let alone our mates. We just have to swallow the humiliation and heartbreak and get on with life, meanwhile, everyone is feeling sorry for our ex and giving her the support we should be getting. Perhaps things will gradually change and a time will come when people will refer to 'that horrid philandress' who dumped her loving husband. I hope so. In the meantime, men need to get a bit more open about their feelings and discuss them with other men. Swap notes in the same way that women do and help each other through the pain and heartbreak of betrayal.

Flexibility

The trouble with heartbreak is that it can sap your strength and cause inertia. We spend all of our time going around in circles and not moving forward. But it's hard to move forward when our hearts are still in the past. We are longing for things long-gone and most likely irretrievable. We also tend to idealise the past, so it becomes this perfect world that we'll never be able to replace. It's a dangerous trap for anyone who has lost something they held very dear. Even more so when the decision was made for them, and not by them.

I'm beginning to realise that there's no such thing as utopia and idealising things or people or situations is unhelpful. If we keep an open mind about life and welcome the uncertainties and actually look forward to its unpredictability, we have a much better chance of getting through it happily. It's impossible to predict anything these days. Covid-19 came from nowhere and changed the world. Curve balls are thrown our way throughout our lives and all we can ever do is deal with them as best we can. Good things happen to us and bad things happen to us and that's life. There needs to be a certain thrill about the future that doesn't scare us but inspires us. It's a matter of letting go of all those safety nets that came with a long-term and—at least what we thought was—stable relationship.

I don't think this is necessarily a stumbling block in terms of committing to a new relationship, it's just a realisation that things do change and we need to be able to adapt in order to survive. From this position of flexibility, we can roll with the punches and the inevitable undulations of life. We can be the wooden building in an earthquake, not the rigid one that collapses. That's the real problem with idealising something or someone, there is no flexibility in our approach and nothing can ever match up to that perfect image we create. Invariably, the image is false and has no basis in truth. But we hang onto it because it was our 'go-to' for so many years. It's more of a habit than something tangible. If we are to move forward successfully, we need to deconstruct the idols in our minds and strip them of their brainwashing capacity. Once we accept flexibility, there is no perfect anything, life just 'is.' I know this is a very Buddhist approach to life, but 'the way things are' is an accepting mantra that can be very helpful.

Of course, it's important to dream too, but only with the caveat that our dreams are flexible too. If we dream about something or someone and things don't go according to plan, so what, that's just the way things are sometimes—much of the time. It doesn't stop us from dreaming, it just makes our dreams a bit more exciting. So, the whole 'letting go' concept is viewed on a bigger canvas and enriches our whole life and not just our view of personal relationships. We become more accepting of change and actually embrace all the chances it can often offer.

Fools Rush In...

Last night, I dreamt about my ex again. It seems no matter how adept I get at blocking out the painful memories of her in my conscious mind, my subconscious sneaks in and reminds me that I still have a way to go. It wasn't one of those dreams that leaves me with a sinking feeling in the pit of my stomach, but it was a sufficiently vivid reminder that my whole being can't stand to be anywhere near her. It was a running away from her dream, not a wanting to be with her dream.

I'm going to need to try and work through this one or else just accept that it will happen and acknowledge that my subconscious mind is still working through things. I should try to view it as nocturnal entertainment rather than any painful reminder. We just have to trust that our subconscious is working for us and not against us. I'm a great believer in the power of the subconscious. Certainly, in a work situation, I've found that it can solve problems if you just leave it to its own devices. Sometimes, we try to overthink things consciously and it leads to brain overload and the computer crashes. The best thing to do is switch it off and fire it up again in the morning, chances are those unsolvable problems will miraculously have sorted themselves out. We need to regularly reboot in order to function optimally.

This diary is so much more than a diary about a failed relationship. It's about getting to know ourselves and learning how we captain this amazing ship. Relationship shit is much like any other shit in our lives and we must fathom out how to deal with it. After my ex's dream, I lay awake thinking about an email I'd sent to a group of colleagues and how not one of them bothered to reply. It was a very heartfelt, but logical offer of help that would see a static situation move forward. My nighttime musings were becoming riddled with resentment and indignation. I was planning an email along the lines of 'if not one of you has had the courtesy to reply to me, stuff the lot of you.' In the past, I've got up and drafted such salvos and then actually sent them. Not a good move. With age has come circumspection. Draft away, but never send. More often than not, what you come up with in the middle of the night will seem extreme and even petty in the morning.

I guess my problem—if it is one—is that I'm an outsider and not an insider. I like to see the big picture rather than the brush strokes. So many of my colleagues are so wrapped up in micro-management and conforming to protocols that they lose sight of what really matters. They are also more concerned with self-aggrandisement than about how a project might build the business. It is so frustrating to see opportunities missed and competitors reaping the rewards. Perhaps, we need to take a more holistic view of ourselves too. How we deal with our relationship issues has the corollary of how we deal with our work issues. If we try to force them and jump in with guns blazing, the results could be pretty messy. Best to take a more measured approach, no matter how difficult it may seem at the time.

Leave the Past Behind

After some relatively euphoric feelings early yesterday and a long purposeful walk along the beach, sad feelings once again crept into my psyche towards the end of the day. It's as if a ten-day high has peaked and it's time to once again slide into the next trough of depression. However, I'm really hoping to buck the trend this time by airing my thoughts here and trying to make sense of them.

Maybe it was one of the characters in a film I watched last night that set me off. She had all the mannerisms of my ex and the beguiling ways. The subtle feelings this woman evoked in me were enough to trigger memories that I couldn't stop myself from visiting. And once you visit one, it's hard not to visit more. I genuinely tried to block these and dislodge myself from those destructive neural pathways, but there is comfort in the pathways despite the impending danger. It's like alcohol, you know it's not good for you but you can't stop yourself from enjoying the temporary good feelings it creates. But just like alcohol, the more you overindulge, the worse you ultimately feel. It doesn't seem to matter how many hangovers you experience, once they've worn off, you still repeat the cycle. It doesn't matter how many times you get dragged down by thoughts of the past and spend days wallowing in deep depression, you still seem to go back there with sickening regularity.

We mustn't. I mustn't. It's ridiculous and a waste of life. The longer we spend in the past, the less time we have for the present. Time is the most precious thing we have because everything else is replaceable. Steve Jobs used to say that we should live every day as if it were our last day. What would we do today, if we knew we were going to die tomorrow? Death is a very levelling thing and something none of us can avoid. It's inevitable. Maybe we should think of it more and put all our other relatively minor hiccups into perspective. Living in the past is robbing us of our precious present, and there isn't any future if we get stuck in this destructive past vacuum.

So, next time you start feeling yourself being sucked into the past vacuum, think about death and the finality of it all. Do you really want to live a living death full of regrets and heartache or do you want to embrace the future and make the very most of those precious years ahead? I know what I want to do and it is something I remind myself of every day. Live in the here and now, not in has-been land. Keep reminding yourself that no matter how much you manage to idealise the past, the future can be so much better if you can only let go. I really thought I was going to die from a broken heart—I sometimes still do—but I won't if I grasp what life has to offer in the here and now. Please don't shut your life down because someone else changed. It was something completely out of your control and something you couldn't change. Beating yourself up with thoughts of 'if only I'd done this' or 'if only I'd done that' is pointless. Just put things into perspective: whether you like it or not, the end of your relationship just happened, but at least you get a second chance to live again. You don't get that with death (and I'm not getting into religious beliefs here). Just think of all those unfortunate people who have had their lives cut short by illness, accident or whatever tragic event. They didn't get a second chance. We do. One world may have come to an end for us, but another even more beautiful one will open up to us if we only give it a chance. Life is precious and we must cherish it and honour it and embrace it with every fibre of our very being. Remember, every day is a last day because we don't get it back. It's up to us to make the most of it. Hug it, embrace it and have fun with it. Most importantly, find another person to share it with. Don't, whatever you do, live a living death by being rooted in the past.

Stop Looking for Answers

Yesterday, I contrasted a failed relationship with death and decided the former is much more preferable. But often we are so depressed at losing someone who has become part of us, even death seems like a valid alternative. It's a terrible thought to even countenance, but for many of us, it has seemed the only option to alleviate the pain. Fortunately, our survival instincts usually kick in and we find a way around that drastic concept—and so we should. We never know what's around the corner and how dramatically our lives can turn out for the better. However, at the lowest points in our grieving process, we often ask ourselves 'What's the point?' What's the point in carrying on an existence that doesn't include the person who seemed to make it all worthwhile? But the important word in that sentence is *seemed*. Once again, our minds latch onto the good times and we forget about the tensions that led to the breakup. We must understand that our soulmate must have been unhappy and seeking something else in order for them to betray us. Like it or not, things weren't working, at least for them.

I have really grappled with this for the last couple of years and still find it very difficult to deal with. Without the same support networks, men find themselves devoid of their one true confidant. It seems that in matters of the heart, men can only really talk to their other half and when she (or he) goes, their emotional support system disappears too. On the other hand, surveys have shown that women are more likely to talk about their emotional issues with close female friends rather than their husbands or partners, so they may have come to some conclusions well in advance of us guys even knowing they were upset. Or, at least, *that* upset. I remember suggesting that my ex talked to her girlfriends as she had sure as hell stopped talking to me. I always imagined the advice she got would be fair and good, but I'm not so sure now. Regardless of external influences upon our former other half, they made the decision themselves to move on and there isn't much we can do about it.

I have also always struggled with the phrase 'the relationship had run its natural course,' but maybe there is more to it than I'm prepared to admit. For me, there was a long way to go, in fact, forever. But it takes two to tango and if one party decides to opt-out, give up and betray the other, maybe it was meant to be. After well over twenty years, there is always predictability about the relationship, it's inevitable. Some couples work through it and reignite the fire, others don't. I guess mine was a case of 'others don't' and that's all there is to it. The fact that I'm still finding the need to write about it does indicate I'm still not over it though. But at least, I'm sounding a little more objective and a degree of acceptance is appearing. I just wish it was a quicker process.

Of course, this diary is about me, but I also want to share my experiences to help anyone out there who is struggling in the same way that I am. Maybe you are fresh out of a failed relationship and are trying to find answers to the questions only time will allow. Time is a great healer, but the phrase doesn't help when you are at a really low ebb. I searched for answers in the early stages and only found regret, disbelief, hurt, anger, sadness and a multitude of other emotional triggers that didn't lead anywhere. The problem is, there aren't any answers. I'm trying to find them and in doing so, I'm making my life a misery. But whoever you are, please stop looking for answers and start looking for opportunities. Everything in life is an opportunity if we only have the courage to see it that way. And yes, it does require courage, because often we are leaving behind the safe and comfortable and heading into unchartered waters. Forget about 'why' we are at this crossroads in our life and concentrate on the massive array of opportunities that lie ahead of us. Stop blaming yourself and your ex and start putting that negative energy into something positive. The future.

What Doesn't Kill You Makes You Stronger

I had a good evening last night but drank too much red wine and it made me a little bit depressed during the night. I lay awake for hours thinking about all sorts of different things. It's as if you are taking stock of your life and trying to find ways of tying up all the loose ends. At one time, I would have fretted about this and my anxiety levels would have increased. These days, I'm more level-headed and accept responsibility for my actions. Nonetheless, I resolved to give the booze the heave-ho for a while. After the euphoric effects have worn off, I think we are more prone to depressive thoughts and that's not good. Hopefully, by writing this intention down in my diary, I can monitor how effective and committed I've been to this decision.

During my hours of sleeplessness, I also thought about topics for this diary, but now I can't remember any of them. I do, however, remember what dream I woke up from. It was a dream about explaining to someone how my marriage had failed and how I made a deliberate decision not to have anything to do with my ex after she left me. This course of action was very hard at the time, but with hindsight, I think it was the right thing to do. Some people stalk their former partners and try to follow them on social media. I think this is a very bad idea because it just keeps the wounds open. It's also sending out a clear signal that despite everything you are still totally preoccupied with this person. Whilst this may well be true for everyone who has been dumped—because we didn't make the decision to leave the relationship—all we are doing is prolonging the agony and not facing up to the devastation this person has caused us. They simply do not deserve our attention or our interest. During the course of my break-up and after my wife had finally admitted that she was having an affair (which had been going on for months, with all the attendant lies and not-so-secret texting), I still told her how much I still loved her and that I was willing to forgive everything if she only stopped seeing the other man. She said 'I love it that you love me' and continued with the relationship despite me pleading otherwise. I remember one particularly heart-wrenching instance when I literally cried and sobbed my heart out for a whole morning. She maintained the cruellest of detachments I have ever experienced in my whole life and still headed off to the meeting her lover was attending. Perhaps, at that point, I knew this wasn't the same person I married. That person would not have been capable of ignoring such devastation. Two and a half years out from that horrendous experience, I still cry occasionally, but it is a far cry from the daily tears I shed for most of the first two years.

In a way, I wish I'd started this diary soon after the separation occurred, but I'm pretty sure it wouldn't have made pleasant reading. Even though a lot of time has elapsed since those catastrophic events happened, those memories are still there but thankfully in a diluted form. I wouldn't want anyone to go through the sheer hell of that period. I know the scars will always be there and despite all my best efforts, there are still triggers that set off waves of pain and regret, but fortunately not so regularly. We really must remind ourselves of the cruelty this person has inflicted on us and that we are better off without them. However, as I mentioned yesterday, there really aren't any answers as to why this situation arose, but it did and our ex felt sufficiently motivated to switch off completely any feelings that remained for us in a very callous manner. I couldn't even contemplate such coldness, but there we go.

I think heartbreak affects people differently and we all have different ways of dealing with it. The recovery (if there is ever total recovery) takes longer for some than others. It may be related to the time the relationship lasted or its intensity. It may have something to do with the personalities of both people. Whatever it is, the process can be excruciating and one of the most emotionally painful experiences in life. It may be an experience we never, ever, expected to happen to us, but once it has, we must learn from it. Remember, whatever doesn't kill you, makes you stronger. Hang in there and please write things down. It's a way of trying to make sense of a whole host of random thoughts that can screw you up if you let them. Don't let your ex keep screwing you up long after they have gone, they simply aren't worth it.

Triggers

In the course of these diary entries, I've tried to cover some of the elements that help us cope when a significant relationship in our life fails. Sometimes, I try to do it subtly, other times, I confront things head-on. But whatever way I do it, I hope it helps. The trouble is, those around us can never *really* know what it's like, because they are not us. They have not had exactly the same life experiences as we have and they probably don't feel things the same way we do. But one thing is for sure, emotional pain is universal and it can drag us into some very dark places if we let it get the better of us.

Today, I want to focus on guilt, because in my half-awake state this morning, I felt the pangs of guilt flow through me when a certain thought went through my mind. Often it is difficult to distinguish between guilt and regret because the waves of emotional pain are very similar. When these states have arisen recently, I've consciously tried to identify what kind of physical feelings they produce. For me, it's a kind of tension in the pit of the stomach or even a stab, since it comes on so quickly. I just mentioned a thought brought it on, but in fact, the feelings can almost arise out of nowhere; it's almost like the state had no particular trigger at all, but just happened spontaneously. Nevertheless, however, it occurred, it's still unpleasant and destabilising. These days, whenever it happens, I use my 'go-to' trick and immediately think of something good, or if I'm on the ball, one of my stock feel-good images comes up on my mind's mental display panel.

I remember reading about neurolinguistic programming in the past and how certain words can elicit certain states of mind. I think it is a very logical explanation of what happens to us when we allow triggers to rule our lives. If we consistently react in a certain way to a particular trigger, we are programming responses that are seldom helpful. It all comes back to Pavlov and his experiments with dogs. Every time Pavlov fed his dogs, he would ring a bell. Initially, the sound of the bell had no connection with the food, but soon the dogs learnt that hearing the bell heralded a tasty meal. They became so programmed that when Pavlov rang the bell, the dogs would instantly start drooling, even if he didn't have any food with him. I just need to hear my ex's name and my blood pressure goes up! Not only that but when I see anyone who looks like her, those waves of regret engulf me in an instant and then maybe guilt and endless other unhelpful emotions pop up too. Let's not become a Pavlovian dog.

I think writing about our feelings in a detached way like this is a different technique to eliminating those gut reactions when they happen in a split second. To avoid those knee-jerk emotional reactions that can lead to endless periods of pain, we must find a way to break the programming pattern. From my experience, that means we must instantly override the trigger with something else. It's like getting the front wheel of your bicycle caught in a groove and being dragged along a predestined path. If that wheel slips into that groove, yank it out immediately and end up in a totally different destination. Every time I see an ex-lookalike, I avert my eyes and think of something completely different. If I don't, I'll be in real trouble and the regret, guilt, longing for past times, and the myriad other things that come as a result of these thought patterns will take over. Stop those thoughts in their tracks.

What started out to be an exposé of the various aspects of guilt has turned into an explanation of how to avoid these feelings. We need to neutralise the triggers, be they verbal, visual or aural. We need to find ways to take the sting out of their tails. In a nutshell, we need to take away their power over us. That is where instant blocking is the only initial solution because it gets us out of those dangerous ruts. If the thought—whether it be visual, word related or an instant feeling—can't get any traction, over a period of time, it will gradually lose its impact, wither away and die. You know what they say, 'If you don't use it, you'll lose it.' Let's not let these triggers use us. Let's not give them the time of day. Instead, create instant counter-triggers that lead to good, positive feelings and a happier day ahead.

Forgive and Forget

I had another dream about my ex last night and I'm wondering if this diary is actually activating parts of my subconscious mind I don't want to be activated! Scary thought. It wasn't a bad dream, quite the opposite. After two and a half years, perhaps, there is a degree of forgiveness creeping in. I guess that isn't a bad thing.

When you imagine you are in a 'forever relationship,' that has already stood the test of time, the idea that it could ever end is unthinkable. It's similar to our view of our parents. If you are fortunate enough to have been brought up in a loving family unit, your parents seem immortal; you simply can't contemplate them not being around. Maybe this is just an explanation of love. If you love someone, you can't contemplate them not being around. I was devastated when my father died, even though I was already in my late 20s. My mother went fifteen years later, but by that time, I was head-over-heels in love with my ex-wife and remained so throughout our marriage. I suppose I had another very deep attachment, so my mother's passing was almost natural. She was also struggling physically and missed my father terribly, so it almost seemed to be for the best at the time.

When someone you really love leaves you through death, the grief is different, because it is final and often unavoidable. When someone you really love leaves you out of choice and then creates a new relationship with someone else, the grief is a lot more complicated. We might regret not telling our parents that we loved them when they were alive, but somehow if it was a healthy relationship, they instinctively knew anyway. They passed away knowing that they will always be in our hearts. The real pain arises when our deep love and devotion are thwarted. What you imagined to be a magical connection that could never be broken, is broken and often in a very cruel way. It is devastating because that connection was severed deliberately. Our parents didn't stop loving us, they

44

just couldn't remain with us in the world. The loving bond with them remains (at least in our minds) forever.

When a partner deliberately decides to turn their back on that magical, mystical bond that has been held in place by rock-solid trust for (often) decades, it's a very hard pill to swallow. The all-encompassing love you gave them is thrown back in your face, it's rubbished and degraded and made out to be insignificant. That's what really hurts. We can cope with the death of a loved one because the love carries on. We can't cope with the betrayal of a loved one because they have clearly indicated their love is not going to carry on. This sort of rejection hits us very, very hard. That's when we start to blame ourselves and question whether our love was/is actually worth anything at all. How could such an intense emotion towards another person be disregarded? How could such a spiritual experience that was shared for so long be trashed? That's when we start to doubt the quality of the other person's love and begin to wonder how much they *really* did love us. Was it all a sham for those years and did we just live a lie? Did we make up this perfect 'match made in heaven' thing when it was actually just one-sided?

Maybe, but we'll never know, or perhaps more importantly, never want to know. Secretly, of course, we will probably always hope that there is still a little corner in their hearts for us. A little area of doubt nags away at them. Certainly, in my own case, my ex said she was torn and even admitted that she could be making the worst decision in her life leaving me. Be that as it may, she went ahead with the decision and chose her new man. I was always honourable and let her make that decision even though it broke my heart. Once she made the decision, I didn't want anything more to do with her. Certainly, face-to-face contact and even correspondence were far too painful to enter into. In the end, the lawyers did everything (at a snail's pace) and she is living her new life and I am living mine. I doubt that either of us will ever be free of this—although she has the ability to bury things a lot better than I do—but I just hope she can live with her decision to break another human being so callously. But I guess when one person changes and the other doesn't, the one who has changed can make up a thousand and one reasons in their own mind to justify their actions. Let's hope they are not lying to themselves as deftly as they lied to us. Where has that forgiveness gone now?

Routes to Happiness

Unfortunately, my resolve lapsed last night and I drank too much wine again. The resultant headache for a lot of the night will certainly put me off overindulging tonight, or better still, not indulging at all, so at least it has one positive…well, kind of. I should learn from the lessons my body is trying to teach me and just do things in moderation. The trouble is, I'm not that sort of guy. It's all or nothing for me in so many areas of my life. But I must try to change or I'll have more sleepless nights ahead of me and more days running at half capacity. That's something of a waste of time which is our most precious gift.

I need to make a conscious decision to change based on past experience: If I drink too many glasses of wine, I'll get a headache and have a bad night's sleep. The trouble is, I forget about the headache quite quickly and then the cycle continues. It's like that with thoughts of our failed relationship. We forget about the bad times and torment ourselves with thoughts of the good times. It's an equally masochistic activity, but sadly, it seldom even contains periods of alcohol-induced euphoria.

When we start thinking back to the good times in our former relationship, it's an easy step to start thinking about the wonderful new life our ex has now made for her/himself and of course, it doesn't contain us. It's another one of those slippery slopes we must avoid. Don't slide into that trap because it's very difficult to escape from it. We must remind ourselves that our ex's personalities will not have changed dramatically since our departure from their lives. All those negative traits that used to drive us to distraction and we ignored—or at least dealt with—because we loved them so much, will still be there. The manipulation techniques, the guilt trips, the criticism, the bullying, the crooked thinking, and the lying, won't have gone away. The only difference is that we no longer have to deal with them because that's now someone else's rotten luck. This is something to celebrate not get sad about.

Honestly, if we put things into this kind of perspective, we will no longer give a damn about what our ex is up to. Even in the unlikely event they changed dramatically once they left us—and this is highly questionable—the fact remains their behaviour whilst they were with us became appalling. There is no point blaming ourselves for this because we loved them as deeply as we always loved them and there was little we could do once their mindset had shifted. I do think we shouldn't try to take responsibility for something that was out of our control. I also think that those very negative aspects of our ex's personality will always be there and that we are well rid of them. We tried to deal with them as best we could at the time and stayed loyal regardless, so what more could we expect of ourselves?

So, when we start to idealise the past and contemplate what we might be missing, we must stop those thoughts in their tracks. Remind ourselves we've fortunately dodged a bullet and some other poor soul will need to deal with that smoking gun. I'm incredibly lucky and have found a wonderful woman who doesn't engage in any of my ex's antics. Life is calm and enjoyable without an eggshell in sight. That's how things should be and if you haven't got to that point yet, keep looking and keep looking forward, not backwards. You won't find any routes to happiness in the past.

Love Is Not About Winning

Good morning, world! Writing a diary about failed relationships has a few challenges, the most important of which is trying to avoid saying the same things over and over again. But quite honestly, I don't think this is really an issue at all because in order to deal with any trauma successfully, we need to visit it and analyse every aspect of it in order to find some closure. Now, I realise I've recommended 'blocking' techniques in the past and I still stand by these when any sort of emotional wave comes over us. This is the only way I know to stop being dragged into unhelpful thought patterns. However, in our more non-emotional and objective moments, thinking through things in a measured and logical manner goes a long way towards long-term recovery.

In my own failed relationship, my ex always wanted to be right; it became part of her personality. She would do anything to achieve this dominant end, including indulging in temper tantrums when she didn't get her own way. She did the same thing with her parents. Being an only child, she was spoilt rotten in one way, but starved of love in another. Her mother (who was an only child) is a cold and detached woman with little innate empathy. She brought her daughter up on a rewards-based philosophy: if she succeeded, she would be given a reward; if she failed, she would be shamed by her parent's disappointment. Her father was more humane but had his own problems being a spoilt only child himself. The temper tantrums were the only way my ex could get attention and the only way her parents would relax their grip. They worked, so why wouldn't she carry on using them in our marriage? I realised early on that I needed to spot the warning signs of an impending storm and release the tension before things got out of hand. It worked and for many years, we had a relatively peaceful life together. Unfortunately, whenever she was in a situation where she could possibly fail, she'd have a panic attack and I'd need to calm her down and try to reassure her that you don't always have to win at everything, you don't always need to be top of the class to enjoy life. In fact, love isn't anything to do with winning, it's something far more overarching than that. I reassured her I would love her whether she was successful or not, I'd love her if we lived in a caravan for the rest of our lives. The problem with my super supportive strategy was that as her confidence grew, the less she needed me. I became redundant. Now, I'm not for one moment suggesting that I was problem-free and I'm sure I brought a heap of hang-ups to the relationship myself. But I do think, towards the end (isn't hindsight wonderful?), my totally supportive and laidback approach left me feeling a trifle undervalued and maybe I became less inclined to acquiesce which led to more frequent tantrums.

Of course, that whole explanation is not about trying to blame my ex for everything, it is about trying to understand an aspect of our relationship that was possibly beyond my control. It was an aspect of my ex's personality that I couldn't do anything to change. I'm quite sure there were aspects of my personality she wanted to change too, but couldn't. In the end, I became a 'yes, dear' man and that wasn't good for either of us. All of these things can creep up over many years and because the process is so slow, you hardly know what's happening. Nonetheless, happening it is and the end result can be heartbreaking. But that's why we are here and all booked in at the Heartbreak Hotel, hoping to find some peace, because we'll probably never find any answers.

Honesty and Friendship

My diary yesterday got rather personal and I'm sorry for that. I have the habit of being very open these days and letting everything out. I became excessively garrulous after my wife left me and poured out all my feelings to whoever would listen. I became an open book as it was the only way I could cope with the heartbreak. I'm still pretty frail when it comes to emotions, even after two and a half years. I can cry at the drop of a hat and easily blub my way through some sentimental movie. 'Pull yourself together man,' I hear you say. Well, I'm trying.

But those expressions of grief are really important and sharing them with people you love can make the difference between surviving and sinking. Most people are very understanding and can imagine the pain you are experiencing. However, they don't really know the half of it until they experience the same sort of grief themselves. When I was happily married, a couple of good friends who had been together for decades broke up and one of the partners came to stay with us and divulged the sad news. I really didn't know what to do and didn't know how to console this woman. In fact, I just couldn't believe what had happened and naively thought it was just a temporary separation and that they'd get back together again when the dust settled. How wrong I was and little did I know I would be facing the same scenario twenty years later. Certain couples seem to be rock-solid on the surface and destined to be together forever. Even their names become inseparable, like Jack and Jill. When the bombshell hits, everyone is dumbfounded and can't quite take it all in. After almost two and a half decades together, I was in that category, and believe me, I couldn't quite take it all in either. But we never aired our dirty laundry in public and always presented a united front, so maybe that's why it was such a shock to the outside world. To be fair, I honestly didn't think we had a huge amount of dirty laundry to air, so that's why it was such a big shock for me too. I guess I must have been delusional. I obviously didn't pick up the signs well enough from within and paid the price.

Be that as it may, I changed post-breakup and became more publicly open about everything in my life. That post-breakup honesty didn't necessarily manifest itself in retaining mutual friends which surprises me, but I think it was the only way I got through that horrible time. I think it broke me emotionally and I realised that honesty is the most important aspect of any relationship. The lies and deceit I experienced hit me hard because I trusted my ex with my life and I never had secrets, I always told her everything. I was an open book to her. I never for one moment imagined she could lie to me, but she did, big time. Fortunately, it hasn't put me off trusting again and I'm still capable of total commitment which is so important in any relationship.

So, what is the moral of today's story? I think it has to be the importance of honesty and the importance of sharing our grief and inner feelings with other people. They may not be able to help in any tangible way, but it is so important for us to unload the burden. Crying is another major tool we must never be afraid to use. It really is amazing how crying can make you feel so much better, because it is yet another release valve. I have shed bucketloads of tears over these years and although the need for them is gradually diminishing, I'm still comfortable having them with me. As a good friend once said to me, "Tears are the language of grief."

Escaping the Chatter

Today is the 18th day of my diary about a failed relationship and the resultant heartbreak that ensues. It has been a very therapeutic experience for me to write about various aspects of this, the most painful period of my life. I just hope that by sharing my thoughts, I will help others along the long road to recovery, either now or in the future. There is no doubt in my mind that it is a long road to recovery for some people and I can certainly speak from personal experience. I just wish I could find a magic wand that we could all use to speed the process up. Years of gut-wrenching torment is not what we want to be signed up for, but can we circumvent some of this pain?

I can't speak for everyone, but in the last few weeks, this daily diary has helped me. Touch wood, I haven't spiralled down into the depths of depression during the whole of this period. There have been a few wobbles and yesterday afternoon, I felt a drop in my spirits that could have been the turning point to the dark side. Luckily, with a good dose of thinking about positive things and blocking any thoughts about my ex and former life, I bounced back and pulled my spirits out of the impending tailspin. It's one more little victory along the recovery highway. All of these little victories add up to an eventual acceptance and ultimate peace of mind.

Peace of mind is definitely what we are after because all of that incessant negative chatter that goes on up top can be very destructive. We go round and round with the same self-deprecating thoughts, recycling events over and over again and getting nowhere. We jump on our hamster treadmill and start running for hours, days and years, trying to get to a destination that doesn't exist. With such negative thoughts, there isn't a destination, there is only a destructive process that is exhausting, demoralising and pointless. Honestly, the only way is to throw yourself off and break the cycle. If we don't break the cycle, we end up backing ourselves into a corner without any sort of escape route and when that happens, the real mental torment begins. We simply *must* give ourselves an escape route.

That's what this is all about, finding an escape route that works. In fact, it might be more than one escape route. Often, it is as much about escaping from ourselves as it is from the situation. Who's responsible for that negative internal chatter? We are. Who's in control of that negative chatter? We are. Well, we could be in control of it if we'd only get off the treadmill and break the cycle. When something traumatic happens in our lives, we tend to go into the default mode of blaming circumstances for the way we feel. We wallow in a 'pity me' scenario because we want people to feel sorry for us. We want the world to know how upsetting this situation is for us. We want the world to know how much this failed relationship meant to us. We want the world to know that we can't cope without this other person in our lives. We want the world to know that we have been betrayed and it wasn't our fault. We want the world to know that we were right and the other person was wrong.

The trouble is, the world generally doesn't give a damn. All of these negative energies are just draining us of the strength to live our lives positively and happily. We are running on the spot and getting nowhere. We are swamping ourselves with emotions that have no meaning in the great scheme of things. We are letting countless different emotions rule our lives because they are all being fired up by the negative chatter in our minds. Chatter=negative emotions=tinges of sadness=depression=chatter=negative emotions=sadness=depression...ad infinitum. We mustn't let the cyclic chatter take hold. Block it and replace it with one of many escape routes. One of mine is obviously writing about such things, maybe it could be one of yours too?

They Aren't Worth It

On my walk yesterday, I decided that today I would write about how our exes can maintain control over us indefinitely if we decide to let them. Love and respect are often words that go together and in any healthy pairing, they form the cornerstone of a long-lasting relationship. The trouble is that when we get dumped, we continue to hold on to these core values (well, maybe less so with the respect part) long after the one who dumped us has moved on. That's because our love and respect for them were genuine, heartfelt and very, very strong—even in the face of their obvious (with hindsight) intentions to move on. This can be a big burden to bear and one that can cause us an immense amount of pain.

They simply aren't worth it. In order for them to dump us in such a cruel manner means that those core values towards us had left them a long time ago. If we continue to carry a torch for them, we are validating something that no longer exists. We are idealising a person who has no feelings for us anymore and someone who hurt us badly. We are giving them power over us when they have lost the right to influence us in any way. By continuing to uphold these core values in a relationship that is over, we are continuing to suffer. They simply aren't worth it and we deserve better.

Unfortunately, genuine love is a very difficult thing to turn our backs on and maybe in some people, it never dies, despite the lack of reciprocation. But we can't let this ruin our lives and our future relationships. Maybe there will always be 'something' about our love that lingers on, even though things ended badly and our heartfelt commitment was rebutted. But we must let that 'something' slowly fade so that it has no influence over our here and now. It is the here and now that matters, not our often-idealised memories of the past. Every moment we spend wallowing in something that has long since gone is a moment wasted. We mustn't allow our ex to continue to have power over us. They simply aren't worth it.

When we break free from this self-inflicted ball and chain, infinite possibilities start to arise. A new relationship will emerge out of the ashes of the old and it will be a hundred times better because it will not be based on lies and deceit. The former person we loved and respected has gone; that person simply does not exist anymore. They killed themselves off when they renounced us. A perfect partnership can't exist when only one person is committed to it. We mustn't hang onto someone who doesn't exist. We must find a new soulmate and leave the past behind. If we don't, we'll never be happy again and that is a terrible waste of life and once again, as far as our ex is concerned, they simply aren't worth it.

The Power of Emotion-Based Memories

Last night, I had another nightmare about my ex and woke up suddenly as she was in the midst of humiliating me. At one time, I'd be in a cold sweat and wouldn't be able to get back to sleep again. These days, I'm much more detached about the whole thing. The emotions that are part of these dreams are still pretty vivid, but I now have the ability to block the thoughts that would otherwise follow. It's a liberating experience and one I'm thankful for. It makes me realise how psychologically damaged I'd become in the relationship and how long those feelings can persist.

Often, we are unaware of what's happening and just carry on in a 'life as usual' routine. The control becomes a part of our lives and we accept it, never dreaming to rock the boat or question the morality of what's happening. I'm not suggesting that every failed relationship has such psychological abuse at its core, but I think there are many that do in varying degrees of intensity. Looking back on my own experience, I now realise how sick I'd become. I'd lost the ability to think for myself and as my ex controlled every aspect of my life, I was trapped in a routine of trying to keep her happy. Sadly, in the end, I was actually afraid of her. She was—and no doubt continues to be—an arch manipulator.

Once we are out of that control zone—and it can take years to extract ourselves fully—we begin to understand what had happened to us. All of our responses were based on the signals we received and they'd become automated. We become like one of those Pavlovian dogs I mentioned in a previous diary entry, reacting to a set of stimuli in a predictable way. You'd think that all of this would end as soon as these people leave our lives, but unfortunately, life isn't that simple. The psychological damage is so ingrained that all the triggers remain in our minds regardless of that person's physical presence. In the early stages of our enforced liberation (when they dump us), every tiny little thing that we experience in our lives has an association with our ex and elicits an emotional response that is catastrophic. Every little thing we see or do prompts a preordained emotional response. That's why we become emotional wrecks—we are being swamped by literally thousands of emotional responses without any let-up. And because all of our most compelling memories are emotionally charged, there isn't even any escape when we're sleeping. The emotions we experience in our dreams are the self-same emotions we experienced originally—that's why dreams can be so vivid.

However, with the passage of time and deliberate resolve to override any of those initial emotional triggers—don't let a vivid dream ignite other firecracker emotional chains—we can begin to deal with things with a certain amount of detachment. We can look at our past life objectively and see what happened. We can begin to acknowledge the psychological damage and make positive steps towards a liberated recovery.

Walking

Today is one of those days when I have no idea what I'm going to write about. I didn't manage my usual walk yesterday, so missed out on a lot of thinking time. In fact, this could be my topic of the day: walking and exercise generally as a way to combat depression. When a bombshell hits us—and we guys are the worst—we tend to lose all motivation to do anything, just being content—or actually unable—to do anything other than possibly drown our sorrows in drink or in some cases, food (I'm reminded of Bridget Jones). With men, our tempering influence has left the relationship, so we often revert to our natural sloppy ways.

Fortunately, in my case, I've always found that walking helps and even after a heavy night on the grog I found the motivation to walk for hours. Walking helped me survive the early months of my heartbreak. On empty beaches crying out aloud, around town crying inwardly, always pushing ahead forcing myself to carry on. Of course, in those early days, my mind was also working overtime trying to make sense of the impossible situation I found myself in. Suddenly, my world had come crumbling down and I didn't know what to do to get it back on track. The person who had been by my side for two and a half decades had turned her back on me. The one person I could confide in and rely on was now forging the same close relationship with someone else (initially behind my back) and had no room for me. The painful phone conversations we had after she left just went round and round in circles. She said she needed time to 'sort herself out' and I said seeing another man was not sorting herself out, but having an affair. I was supposed to hang about for six months whilst she did this kind of 'sorting herself out.' The six months trial separation she suggested was simply a safety net for her in case her new relationship didn't work out. It was hideous. However, despite that, I remained faithful to her up until the very day she told me there was no going back a couple of months after I ceased to have any contact with her. Contact was pointless because we just went around in the same ridiculous circles. I also knew I needed to be away from her manipulative ways.

When I said I couldn't sleep and was very, very depressed, she advised me to see a doctor, get some sleeping pills and go on antidepressants. Thanks a bunch. I think I'll just keep walking. But that is two and a half years ago and I'm still here and in a much better state of mind. It has been a very long and painful process though and one I wouldn't wish on anyone. In the early stages, however, I just couldn't imagine having any life at all after she left. My life was empty and desolate. We did everything together and had done so for years. But maybe that was part of the problem and one I've talked about elsewhere. Regardless of that, we must always find a way to carry on. We must find a way to think positive thoughts and block out the negativity.

With hindsight, my advice would be to block out any thoughts of your ex as much as possible, because if you don't, you'll be going round and round in circles for the rest of your life. I've been there and done that and I'm only now beginning to understand I should have used my blocking techniques from the very start and kept them up. Regurgitating the same negative thoughts over and over again just led me to continuous heartache and a very depressing life. As I said the other day, your ex is simply not worth it.

My apologies for this dog's breakfast of a diary entry, but I'll try to do better tomorrow. In the meantime, if you are suffering, please don't forget to eat well, drink in moderation and get plenty of exercise; you'll be in better shape to cope with anything if you do.

Acceptance (1)

I dreamt about my ex again last night. It wasn't a very long dream, but it was a kind of warm fuzzy one that had a sad ending. It was all about trying to locate her at a bus station and when I did, I found the wonderful woman I married all those years ago. Fresh-faced, honest and so loving. I say the dream was sad because when I saw her, she smiled and I started to cry and that's when I woke up. I told you it was a short sad dream.

My mother used to say 'She's got it bad' when referring to our courtship days. I certainly caught the love bug too—in a big way—and 'got it bad.' I think what we need to understand from these dreams is that we are hanging onto a perfect memory, an idealised version of our ex that—as I said yesterday—no longer exists. The tears are for a lost love that has long since gone. Fortunately, this dream wasn't a painful experience and I didn't wake up in a panic. I just woke up and smiled. The kind of smile you smile when you think about something warm and fuzzy. As long as our memories become benign, I think we are on the road to recovery. As long as we can view them for what they are—something that won't exist again—we can think of them fondly and smile.

I used to have lots of dreams about losing my ex and with hindsight they were prophetic. Maybe deep down, I knew our relationship was doomed. Although it certainly didn't seem like that at the time. Maybe I thought she was too good for me and I became master of my own fate? Who knows, I don't. Ultimately, it is what it is and there isn't much I can do about it. However, what I can do is become accepting of the situation and learn to live with it. In fact, make it my friend and not my foe. Everything in life changes and no matter how much we try to keep things the same, we can't. Physically, we can't do the things we used to do, so we must adapt and accept them. Mentally, we probably can't do the things we used to do, so we must adapt and accept. Acceptance is one of the most important things to enjoy a happy life.

My wonderful new partner is very accepting of my need to write a diary. For the last two years, she has witnessed my heartbreak and the resultant deep, deep depression which accompanied it. She has heard about every painful part of my breakup and offered me an endless supply of love and support—she is an amazing woman and I am incredibly lucky to have her in my life. I often feel very guilty about spending time thinking about my past rather than thinking about her. But this is a process I just need to go through and she very kindly understands that. As every day goes by, the acceptance becomes more natural and that's the way it should be. Even my dreams have a certain acceptance about them. If we can all smile at thoughts of the past, we can be sure that we are accepting it, not with bitterness, but with a groovy kind of love.

The Blues

I almost didn't want to write an entry today as I had a touch of the blues just before going to sleep. It doesn't take much to go from a touch of sadness to full-blown depression. When we know the trigger, we can block the thoughts that logically move on from it, but when it's just a vague feeling, that's a bit harder. This morning, in another context, I was thinking about the phrase comparing apples to pears and immediately my mind went to the pear tree I planted on the grounds of the wonderful house I shared with my ex for many, many years. It would have been a very easy segue from the garden to the house to the happy times and to ultimate deep depression. But I'm not going there and haven't been there since I started this diary. So, what do we do about those vague feelings, or are these just a part of the usual ups and downs of life?

I'm not so sure how to answer that last question. I guess life comes with a certain amount of fluctuation. It is made up of varying degrees of opposites. Light and dark, hot and cold, fast and slow, happy and sad. But I'm still sure it's possible to remain more in the happy zone rather than the sad zone if we make a conscious effort. Even if one of those blue feelings comes over us, we can (a) try to identify where it came from—and there usually is a very subtle trigger—or (b) resolve to replace it with something uplifting. Having been through so much sadness in recent years, I'm literally over it because I know how destructive it can be. There is a great book called *You Can't Afford the Luxury of a Negative Thought* and what better statement could there be than that? We can't afford it because it saps us of so much of our strength and those kinds of luxuries can actually make us ill.

It really doesn't matter whether we are talking about a failed relationship, failed friendship, failed business, failed exam or failed anything. The answer is always to move on but learn from the experience. There are countless examples of successful business people, entertainers, inventors, writers…you name it…who have struggled, hit rock bottom and had to rebuild their lives. In fact, in the business world going bankrupt seems to be almost mandatory for ultimate success. Fall down seven times and pick yourself up eight. That's good advice. We must always have faith that whatever life throws at us, we will deal with it and not only deal with it but make the most of the opportunity. If we view everything in life as an opportunity to reinvent ourselves, we'll keep moving forward and discovering endless new possibilities. That's where we simply must deal with those blue moments constructively and move on from the feelings rapidly. Any wallowing and we won't have the energy to get up that eighth time. You see, I'm glad I made the effort to write this, rather than wallow in a blue feeling that didn't seem to have any genesis. If I'd given in and not moved on, I'd sure as hell have found something to feel miserable about. We are all little children; we need a distraction from our pain. Our life is full of tiny little learning dramas which we never remember individually but they all go to make up who we are. The trick is to get over them as quickly as possible and move on. With enough practice, moving on becomes second nature and our ability to substitute blue thoughts with good thoughts becomes almost instantaneous. I'm aiming for that kind of enlightenment. I may have a way to go, but I'm sure it's the best way forward.

UoL

Yesterday was a good day after writing about those blue feelings. I think this writing lark certainly works. If we don't have some form of release valve for all those pent-up thoughts, the mind becomes a bit jumbled. It's an amazing thing, the human brain, the most sophisticated computer on the planet. In fact, there isn't a computer in existence that can match its complexity. The beauty is we all have the same gismo sitting on top of our shoulders, so our options are much the same across the board. In one form or another, we all face the same challenges too, no matter how rich or poor we are. It's a levelling thought, but also a comforting one too. It's so easy to imagine that it's just us going through these feelings of heartbreak and rejection, but actually, almost everyone will face the same feelings at some time in their lives.

No matter how rich you are, how educated you are, or how worldly-wise you think you are, when a bombshell hits, we become the same fragile human beings struggling to cope. It's as if emotions are beyond our control, something you can only learn about at the University of Life (UoL). These University of Life courses just seem to go on forever. Just when you thought you'd passed every paper there is, the UoL alters the syllabus and gives you another hurdle to jump. We all deserve PhDs at the end of it all. But life is like that and provided we accept this we'll always be learning until the end of our days; we'll always be prepared for anything. We live in an age of fluidity, where nothing in life is secure. There is no such thing as job security, no such thing as health security and obviously for us, no such thing as relationship security. Or is there?

Certainly, in the realms of relationship security, we can learn from our mistakes. Often, it's a matter of not taking things for granted, and not becoming too comfortable in the safe space we feel we're in. This is particularly true of long-term relationships when the two people know each other so well, they begin to take each other for granted. It's the Jack and Jill scenario I talked about a few entries back. With my ex, I felt that we were in something that was going to last for the rest of our lives. I actually believed the 'till death us do part' stuff. Naive or what? It took a bombshell to repudiate that concept. But at least I've passed another one of those UoL papers. The knowledge I've gained is helping me appreciate how lucky I am in my new relationship. It is making me realise that we all need to work on a relationship and we need to keep learning and adapting along the way.

That's all a part of growing as a human being; it's all a part of this endless learning process that will last for the rest of our lives. Sometimes, we have to study ourselves as much as anything external. We need to learn the best way to cope with those emotional things that books can't tell us about. It's all practice-based and rarely theoretical. That's what I've been doing for the last two and a half years and I'm still learning. I've been adapting and experimenting and thinking and doing, trying to find the best way to cope with the new course I wasn't prepared for. The most demanding one I've ever had to pass at the University of Life. I've tried to share some tips to help you get through this paper too, but I guess, we all need to approach it differently and can only really write our own study guide. Good luck, we'll all pass in the end.

Ups and Downs

I hope there will come a stage in my life when I can look back on the two and a half decades I spent in my previous relationship and value some of the memories. Of course, at the moment, it's still too painful. The memories are too raw and I know if I dip into them, I'll get engulfed in a torrent of associated emotions. But given time, maybe I'll be able to pick a few out and enjoy them. I hope so. It would be a shame to have to bury a large chunk of my life, rather than savour it. I guess that's where relationship breakups cause so much damage and why they are so sad. You share so much with someone for so long and then you need to put it behind you. However, not only are you putting the good memories behind you, but you are also having to forgo the chance to share them with the other person who helped create them. 'Remember the time we did this?' or 'Remember the time we did that?' Twenty-plus years of shared memories and then nothing, it's hard and a wee bit tragic.

Of course, not all failed relationships end in complete detachment. Sometimes, the couple manages to remain friends, despite going their separate ways and finding new partners. Maybe that sort of separation was more amicable and didn't involve the kind of lies and deceit that mine did, in which case, I can only feel happy for them. In my case, if only those lines of communication had stayed open who knows what might have been possible? Sadly, they didn't and my ex became my judge, jury and executioner before I knew anything about it. When I did, it was all too late, she was already in a new relationship and wouldn't even give our marriage a chance by going to counselling. That's a bit sad, but not necessarily her fault. When emotions are involved, we seldom do the rational thing; sometimes, we are driven by frustration and desperation. Moreover, sometimes we are driven by the thrill of something new and the immense amount of attention we are suddenly getting. Not that I know anything about that because I wasn't in her position, I was the one trying to make sense of the betrayal. To be honest, I don't think I'll ever make sense of that because I could never have treated her in the same way. I just couldn't have hurt her and lived with myself. That of course all sounds holier-than-thou and doesn't really help very much.

We all make decisions in life based on the information we have at the time and also based on the emotional state we are in. And then there is the change factor to figure in as well. But can we really change so dramatically? I'm not so sure. We must make a conscious decision to change and accept the consequences. Maybe we can convince ourselves that our actions are justified and not really care about how much they impact the other person. That certainly seemed to be the stance my ex took. Because I have ceased to have any contact with her whatsoever, she is oblivious to the length of time it is taking me to recover. Maybe that is for the best.

This is probably another reason why relationship breakups that are not amicable seldom lead to continued life-long friendships. The pain lingers on for far too long for the betrayed party. Only time will tell if I can at least revisit some memories from those two and a half decades, but one thing is for sure, I don't think I'll ever be able to have any personal contact with my ex ever again.

Writing this diary is all about mapping mood fluctuations and today's is hopefully just one aspect of it. I don't want to sound negative because that is the one thing we should all be trying to avoid. Everything is a process and the process consists of all sorts of ups and downs. We need to be accepting of both.

Questions and Decisions

I haven't had a particularly good run of entries recently. I've felt a bit dissatisfied with the content and the way I've expressed myself. I imagine that is the fate of every writer as there will be good days and there will be bad days. But I'm determined to box on regardless. For me, this is all therapy and one therapy that doesn't come out of a wine bottle; now that's real progress.

In five days' time, I will have been writing this diary for a month and that is a month without any major depression slumps. Now, that's progress too and something to really celebrate. Depression is a killer, it just saps everything out of you and you begin to wonder what life is all about. I've done that a lot in the last few years. I've been in so many dark places I began to question whether there would ever be light at the end of the tunnel. A lot of that questioning was self-directed. Have I actually achieved anything worthwhile in my life? The thing I was most proud of was my marriage and that just disappeared before my eyes in a very short space of time. Will life ever be the same again? Well, of course, it won't be, but that doesn't mean it can't be just as good, and in many ways so much better.

The trouble with all those sorts of questions is that they increasingly add value to something that no longer exists. It's one of those personal torture techniques that everyone who is hurting indulges in. In a way, it's part of human nature. To be fair on ourselves, part of the questioning has come about because what we considered to be sacrosanct wasn't held in the same high regard by our ex. We are questioning our judgement and our ability to read people. When you think you know someone inside out and they then turn on you, it kind of knocks you off balance. You then start to question every decision you've made in your life and question your ability to make good decisions in the future.

But we are being far too hard on ourselves. When we got married, we based that decision on the way we were then. Both of us were completely different people in a completely different time zone. It was the right decision at that time, regardless of what transpired. We also subsequently enjoyed many happy years together, so that's a good result. We must try to celebrate our past rather than regret its passing. I'm a great believer in core values and I don't think my core values have changed much over the years. I believe in equality and respecting other people's views and opinions even if they don't happen to be my own. I also want to help people whenever I can. I never imagined that anyone with the same core values could ever change, but I think they can. Just because I haven't changed doesn't mean that all the people around me don't change either. They can and do. When we start to question ourselves in such a rigorous way, we are doing it on the basis that all things remain equal, but in fact, they don't. We are not still on the same level playing field. We are now on a football field and someone has moved the goalposts. Once we start to acknowledge that there are certain things in our life that are completely beyond our control, we can stop blaming ourselves and questioning every decision we've ever made.

With such a positive view of our decisions, it's also possible to move forward faster. Some of the most worrying times in life are when we can't make a decision to do anything. We get trapped in that limbo land of indecision. Shall I, shan't I, will I, won't I. We spend sleepless nights worrying about making the right decision and the whole process becomes a nightmare. We endlessly put things off and because of this procrastination become increasingly agitated. It's another form of torture. Once we finally make a decision and go with it, life becomes so much more enjoyable.

The important thing is to make a decision based on the available evidence and then stick to it. There is no right or wrong and whatever happens, it will be a learning experience and if we choose to view it as such we can't go wrong. As long as we bear in mind that there will always be things beyond our control, we can avoid all of those pesky questions of self-doubt. Once we learn to accept outcomes for what they are—learning experiences—we can get on with our lives and make the very most of them.

Pride and Prejudice

My ex's favourite book and TV adaptation (featuring Colin Firth) was Pride and Prejudice. The story involves depicting the two prominent male characters in stark contrast: Darcy is proud and principled and Wickham is a liar and a scoundrel. Darcy keeps all of his good deeds to himself and is therefore initially viewed as cold and unkind. Wickham, however, charms everyone with his superficial good nature. The truth eventually comes out and good overcomes evil. Honesty and integrity win over lies, deceit and avarice. I like that allegory. I hope my ex watches it again and picks up the message this time.

I have never enjoyed any form of confrontation and much prefer to turn the other cheek and walk away. In my view, unless someone is prepared to start the compromise process, nothing can be achieved to resolve a conflict. Unfortunately, like Darcy, our good nature can go unrewarded and superficial lies and chatter swamp our good deeds. It is hard to remain strong and retain our dignity in these situations. It is hard to remove ourselves from the mud-slinging and end up being labelled the protagonist in any relationship split or at the very least have to accept the lie that the split was mutual. It goes against the grain and is a bitter pill to swallow. I do know that doing the honourable thing has cost me a lot of friends. I know that by cutting myself off from the mud-slinging when it was about to gain traction left my side of the story untold. Silence became an admission of guilt and my initial honest explanation of events to every one of our mutual friends was lost in my ex's zeal to be right. But so be it. I have long been of the opinion that the truth will always come out, but more importantly, I retain a clear conscience in the meantime. Friends come and go, but principles founded on honesty and integrity must stay with you for life.

With hindsight, towards the end, I think my ex did everything in her power to push me away. She tried to make me leave her so that she didn't have to leave me. It would have been the ultimate 'face-saving' device. She could have remained righteous to the outside world without having to continue the lies and deceit publicly. I remember that after she left the family home, she was at real pains to stop me from telling the neighbours the truth. She didn't want them to know she'd had an affair and was leaving me. She said it might impinge on her business. What hypocrisy. However, because I still loved her, I told the truth, but would never divulge any of the sordid details.

In the end, it didn't really matter. She could continue to spin her webs of deceit and present herself to the world as the long-suffering wife who left a marriage that had run its course. She could also tell everyone it was a mutual decision. When I was still in touch with mutual friends and this line of events came back at me, I'd have to gulp very hard, flush with indignation and just bite my tongue. I didn't want to go down that track as it ends up nowhere, but involves a hell of a lot of pain for both of us on the way. In the end, I walked away from those friends and have avoided having to face that nonsense ever since. I've upheld Darcinian principles and I'm proud of it. I get to tell my story here, anonymously. My former friends can think what they like about me, but I'm remaining true to myself. Unlike my ex, I'm not interested in whether the world thinks I'm right or wrong, but I am interested in retaining my own core values. I'd much prefer to be Darcy than Wickham.

Look on the Bright Side

Good morning, world! It is always good to celebrate a new day and look forward to the opportunities it will present. Because the opportunities will certainly be there if we choose to find them. Life is a very precious thing and something we should never take for granted. This morning, I woke up to the sad news that someone I had met a couple of times on holiday had passed away. She was a lovely lady, very gentle and kind and a great reader. I will write a message to her husband later today with my condolences. I haven't seen them for quite a number of years but I am sad I will never see her again, at least not in this world.

In this writing adventure of mine, I've tried to tackle all manner of issues related to a failed relationship and the kind of fallout it produces. It's been a process of airing random thoughts about heartache, emotional pain and ultimately acceptance. I have found myself being vitriolic on many occasions and for that, I apologise. I realise I am not a perfect person by any means. I am tarred with the same brush as those I accuse and often when the bitterness gets hold of me, I fail to offer a balanced opinion. But we are all human and we must be accepting of our own weaknesses as much as those around us. No matter how fair we hope to be, we often lash out as a means of self-protection. We are trying to maintain some semblance of self-respect in the wake of a traumatic event. In the midst of it all, it's very difficult to be fair and measured. But once the worst of the storm is over, hopefully, we can all return to a more balanced view of events and start to enjoy all that life has to offer.

I would really encourage anyone who reads this to start their own daily diary, just as a means to clarify all the thoughts that buzz around. It doesn't need to be anything flash (and mine certainly won't win any literary awards), but sometimes it really helps to get things off your chest. It is also a good way to remind yourself of the things that help you avoid the slippery slope into depression. As I've said in the past, spending two-and-a-bit years (or however long it may be) in the depths of despair and often at the point of giving up, is a terrible waste of life. If we can get some of those negative thoughts out on paper and look at them objectively, hopefully, it will help us to move forward. I have found this daily writing experience immensely therapeutic and for reasons I don't even understand. For me, just waking up and starting to write clears my mind for the day, and truth be told, it actually stops me from focusing on dangerous thought processes that lead to depression. It also helps to consolidate the techniques I've found useful to avoid depression. Whenever I start to slip into thoughts about my past, an internal alarm bell goes off with big red flashing lights that read 'Don't go there.' Having 'been there' thousands of times in the past few years, I realise that it is a very destructive place to be in. It saps energy, creates worry and makes your heart bleed. It also achieves nothing at all but pain.

My advice from my experience is to avoid those dark places and look for the light. If you want to visit anything about your former relationship, visit it in a detached way like this. Write about it as an observer rather than a participant. Try and see both sides of the story even if you end up just stating your own. Stating our own side of the story is good for us because we need to feel that we still have value whatever happened. We do still have value and we still have a great life to lead if we only choose to lead it. Life is full of amazing opportunities if we can only clear our minds of the past, concentrate on the now and be excited by the unexpectedness of the future.

Liberation

On Friday, I will celebrate a month of writing this diary. There have been some really good entries, some moderately good ones and some downright awful ones. If you have followed me all the way along this momentous journey, thank you so much for your company. If I have managed to help, amuse or just pass the time of day, I'm glad, that's enough for me. As I mentioned in my entry yesterday, writing all of these thoughts down has helped me enormously. Somehow, I seem a lot stronger and better able to deal with life in general. It may simply be that after two and a half years of heartache, I'm finally coming to terms with this most dramatic part of my life. It might be that the gut-wrenching heartache is over and I may never spiral down into those awful depths of depression ever again. I hope so. However, they do say it takes a month for new habits to take hold and new neural pathways to be formed, so maybe my writing therapy is finally working.

I think I got into the habit of expecting any periods of feeling good about myself to be followed—as a matter of course—by feelings of complete desperation. It was as if the cycle was predestined and I had absolutely no control over it. In a way, I was frightened about feeling good, because I knew it wouldn't be long before I felt bad again. It was similar to those very early days when I was afraid to go to sleep because I couldn't face waking up to the same nightmare. It's a sickness for sure and a tragic reflection of who I was after my marriage ended. I was brainwashed into thinking my life had ended when my marriage ended. I don't know if I brainwashed myself or if my ex had a hand in it, but brainwashed I was for sure. It's an appalling state of mind to be in and one I hope I will never face ever again.

I know it's a cliché, but time is a great healer. I'm reluctant to say that because whenever I read the countless online 'how to get over a breakup' articles, I often got annoyed with them because they all seemed so matter-of-fact and clinical. It was a coldness that just didn't seem to fit with my situation. How on earth could I put such an important emotional bond of 24 years behind me in such a flippant way? It was impossible at least for me at that time. Maybe if I'd been with that person for 24 months, but not 24 years. Sorry, but I also couldn't cope with the kind of detachment a lot of the women who were writing these articles displayed. They seemed to me to be just like my ex, totally devoid of feelings. They could stand back, be completely objective and say 'You'll get over it.' Well, maybe they were right because I am getting 'over it.' But the process has been immensely complicated and painful. Having said that, I am even beginning to forget the pain to a large extent.

I think what I'm trying to say is that emotional trauma takes quite a while to deal with and no doubt the scars will always be there in one form or another. What I would love to say is that I don't think you need to spend the same amount of time as I have dealing with it. I don't want you to be in the same no man's land (two and a half years) when you don't have to be. Until recently, I think I have dealt with this emotional trauma the hard way. I have tried to face it head-on by thinking about it all the time. For at least two years, it completely preoccupied my mind. Every thought I had concerned my ex. Everything I looked at, heard or experienced, made me think of my ex. It was all-consuming and obsessive. It was a kind of morbid fascination in emotional pain. It was a cycle of painful thoughts full of regret and longing. It was a complete and utter emotional sickness that I didn't seem to be able to extract myself from.

I honestly think that I could still be in this trap, but I'm not now. I'll try to explain more tomorrow…

Be in Control of Your Own Destiny

I said yesterday that I could still be in that up-and-down cycle if it hadn't been for this diary. I think it's true. By writing my thoughts down, I have confirmed in my own mind that any weakness in terms of backward thoughts is catastrophic. If I allow myself to be seduced into taking thought pathways that lead to memories of my marriage, I'm doomed. I did that for over two years and it led nowhere. Well, actually it did lead somewhere, it led to deep bouts of depression. My whole mindset is beginning to change. Not only am I refusing to rake over anything in my past that involves my ex, but I am also refusing to rake over anything that might depress me. I am also refusing to worry about things that might never happen. The future is something to look forward to, rather than fret about. I have decided that whatever happens, I'll deal with it. Unlike other times when I've decided to do this, on this occasion, it all seems to be more organic. The other times have been brought about by reading lots of self-help books which only seem to offer temporary relief. In no time at all, the positive thoughts cycle into negative ones and I'm back to square one. This time, things are different.

We only get one chance with life and we mustn't spend it destructively. It's a precious gift to savour, not to squander. If the traumas of the last few years have taught me anything, they have taught me the value of living in the here and now and not wallowing in the past or expecting too much of the future. By all means, we should have dreams, but nothing that is going to cause us heartache if they become unfulfilled; that is another form of slavery. Plan and then adapt. Likewise, we need to have the flexibility to accept any mistakes we make on the way. We are only human and if every now and then, we make a wrong decision, so be it, we just accept it and learn from it. No recriminations and no scolding. We must try to find the positive side in everything.

I honestly never thought I would be in such a good space after all that has transpired in the last few years. My life seemed to be in a mess and I felt there was no way out of it. I was riddled with self-doubt and unable to make any decisions without second-guessing myself. I was a possum caught in the headlights of an oncoming truck, not knowing whether to go left, or right, or just retreat. I was frozen and powerless and backed into a corner by indecision. It was a terrible place to inhabit. Please don't go there, because you don't need to.

Whatever you do, don't let other people make decisions for you. Don't let anyone else have that sort of power over you. If they want to control you, they are not looking after your best interests, but their own. If we become reliant on them and then they suddenly pull the plug, our lives come crashing down around us and we end up (like me) going through hell trying to rebuild everything from scratch. We might convince ourselves we are doing the right thing because we love these people so much, but what seems to be a sacrifice to please them, is actually suicide for us. Towards the end of my marriage, I became so controlled by my wife, I was incapable of making any decisions myself without checking with her. This was after years of making decisions and being chastised for them. It was so destructive and not something I ever want to experience again. Being ruled with a rod is not good for anyone. Unfortunately, what starts off with us simply trying to please the other person ends up with us becoming impotent. It is life-sapping and very, very dangerous.

One of the reasons my life was in tatters after my wife left me was because of this total inability to think for myself. Ok, fortunately, I had enough inbuilt survival instincts to keep moving forward after the bombshell and that fuelled my dating site escapades, but when I eventually found someone, I was still mentally controlled by my ex. I was incredibly lucky to find someone who genuinely understands what I had been through and how mentally sick I was. She has stuck by me and has helped me to rebuild my self-confidence. I am now beginning to be able to make decisions again and it's so liberating. I am beginning to get my life back and become a real human being, not someone else's punching bag. I can't tell you how wonderful that is.

So yes, I think it is possible to recover from a broken heart and from a relationship that was actually quite toxic. The trouble is, we don't think it's toxic when we're in it. If you are like me, you think love conquers everything and you stay loyal and devoted no matter what is thrown your way, no matter how much you are manipulated. Even when this person dumps you and buggers off with someone else, you are still 100% committed and that's the problem. You blame yourself and beat yourself up. You live in a living hell for years and if you are lucky to find a new partner as I did, they have to cope with your heartbreak too.

As I said, I've been incredibly lucky to find an amazing woman who was willing to help me pick up the pieces and reconstruct my life. We all have to have confidence that person exists. We also need to stick to our core values and not turn into the person our ex has become. If we remain honest, kind, caring and trustworthy, we'll attract the same sort of person and our lives will be transformed. However, having learnt from our previous experience, we will NEVER allow ourselves to be controlled by anyone ever again.

Onwards and Upwards

Today is exactly a month since I started writing this diary. If you have been with me for the whole time, I'd like to thank you for your fortitude. Throughout the course of this experiment, I have been at pains to point out that most of the benefit comes to me because it helps me to sort out a hell of a lot of things in my mind. But regardless of that, I really hope that by sharing my thoughts, I am providing a few ways forward for other people as well, either now or in the future. I've certainly learnt a lot about myself and about how to cope with some painful experiences.

In yesterday's entry, I was marvelling at being in a good space mentally after nearly a month without any major periods of depression. Well, actually no periods of depression at all. This is a major breakthrough for me and one I'm attributing to writing my thoughts down. That, and actually putting all that I preach into practice. I've talked about blocking out images or trains of thought that lead to my ex. I've talked about letting go of mutual friends who remind me of my ex. I've talked about thinking about the whole business but remaining emotionally detached from it. I've talked about so many things that make me a stronger person. I just hope that by airing such things in a diary like this, all of these things might strike a chord with you too.

When I first started writing these diary entries, I was well on the way to recovery. I'd already spent two and a half years in a terrible pain zone, so I'd done my time. But no matter how much I tried, I'd still allow myself to drift back into my past and scratch the scars. In fact, I'd scratch them so much, they'd often start to bleed. Since writing, I've consciously avoided any of this and although I've described events in some detail, I have always blocked any emotional memories completely. Memories as such are fine, it's the emotional memories that are the real killers. Once in a while, I've mentioned my ex popping up in dreams and there have been good and bad experiences there. But even when the dreams were emotionally charged, I always avoided following them up with emotionally charged recollections. It really is working for me.

I think I have also set myself a challenge. I've challenged myself to remain upbeat and positive for as long as possible. In the past, I'd be in and out of depression every couple of weeks, and as I said yesterday, I became suspicious of my good spirits because I knew they would be followed by their opposites. It's crazy thinking, to be afraid to be happy because you know you'll be sad soon afterwards. I'm not suggesting that now I'm going to be living in a euphoric state for the rest of my life, but what I am feeling is the sense that deep depression can be a thing of the past. We all experience sadness and when we are in a good mental state, we realise it will be a transitory state. Deep depression is so different and the kinds of deep depression I've experienced have made me utterly powerless and unable to function as a normal (whatever that is) human being. Maybe most people have reached this level of enlightenment already and I've just been living in a dark world for far too long.

I'm determined to keep these good spirits up. I'm determined to emphasise the positive and eliminate the negative. Every seemingly negative aspect always has a positive side to it if we look hard enough. When our spirits are high, it's easier to find those positive slants in a situation, when we are down it's almost impossible. Block out the negative and keep away from negative people, they can be very infectious.

So, after 30 or so diary entries, I'm celebrating the positive and eliminating the negative. Whatever I do, I'm going to block those memories of my ex. I might never be able to open that box of emotional memories and that's fine because I'm better off without them. They have already cost me an enormous amount of time and they could drain me for the rest of my life if I let them. We are all worth more than this. The ex has moved on a long time ago, now it's my turn and your turn too if you are in the same position. Onwards and upwards!

Take a Risk on Life

It's 4.10 am in the morning and I can't sleep. I decided to get up and start to write in the hope that I might have something interesting to say, or at the very least, clear my mind of the various thoughts that have been buzzing around for the last hour or so. It's not that the thoughts have been destructive, it's just that they've been keeping me awake. These days, I'm trying to keep my thoughts firmly focused on the future and not be tempted to go into that department in my brain that concerns my ex. This diary has been all about blocking out that compartment of my life and moving forward. Having said that, it has also been about looking back on the course of events objectively and trying to make sense of what happened, even if there doesn't seem to be any sense there at all.

Today is the dawn of another month of diary entries. It could well have been the sunset, but instead, I've decided to continue on my quest to stay sane. I've shared a lot of thoughts over the last month and quite a few personal details about my life. It has been a cathartic experience and one that I wouldn't want to turn my back on. These are observations for myself as much as observations for the wider world. But that's fine and God forbid I become like one of those Facebook people who post details of their extremely tedious daily lives. I really don't give a damn about that sort of crap, although I sometimes think who gives a damn about the sort of crap I've been writing about recently! At least I'm honest and not fooling myself that I have anything particularly earth-shattering to offer the world.

You know what? At one time, I was quite concerned about what I could offer the world. I was always striving to be the best I could be in my profession. After every qualification I gained, I'd always be looking towards the next. On and on in the mistaken belief that gaining qualifications made me a more valuable person. It was a way of seeking validity. Part of this must have its roots in my upbringing. My father didn't make it to university even though he had a very sound schooling thanks to gaining a scholarship. He spent the rest of his life feeling on the back foot of everyone with a degree. It was sad and unnecessary but obviously had an unconscious influence on me. I became a qualification junkie, always thinking that by gaining the next degree or diploma I'd be guaranteed success. How wrong I was. It's not qualifications that make you successful, it's confidence and the ability to make the most of every situation you find yourself in. It's also a matter of determination—but at least in that respect, I had the determination to finish everything I started.

With hindsight, I think we all need to be service-based, not self-based, and in a way, I'm still the latter rather than the former. If I spent more time promoting what I write, I might be helping more people. But there again, the insecurities start to creep in and you wonder if your random thoughts are actually of interest to anyone but yourself. Weird or what? The funny thing is that most of the most successful people in the world have had to struggle too. Their story is never one of plain sailing from rags to riches (or from riches to riches in Donald Trump's case), it always involves a struggle. The number of ultimately successful manuscripts that were initially turned down is legion. The number of inventors who were told their ideas were ridiculous is in the same category. We all need to keep striving no matter what pushback we get because we simply don't know which pushback could be the penultimate before ultimate success. But what is success anyway? My idea of success could be totally different from yours. In my field, it's public recognition and of course, recognition from your colleagues. However, is there actually a difference between professional success and personal success?

At one point in my life, I thought I'd got everything covered. I had achieved qualifications and a degree of professional success. I also had a long-lasting marriage to someone I was deeply committed to. Someone I really loved and someone whom I would never have betrayed. It was the fairy tale partnership that was the most important thing in my life. It was my life; it was as precious to me as life itself. But somehow, it didn't remain that way for my wife and she decided to jump ship. Maybe I wasn't successful enough for her. Maybe if I'd poured more energy into my own career and less into promoting hers, things would have been different. Who knows and it really doesn't matter now. You can only do your best at any given point in time and what will be, will be. There is always going to be a randomness about life that we can't control.

As an epilogue to today's ramble, I'd just like to remind myself and anyone that might be reading this, that we don't get out of life alive. Most of us don't know when we will shuffle off this mortal coil and that's probably a good thing. But if we spent every moment of our lives worrying about our impending departure, we'd never do anything. Life is a risk and we'll always regret the things we didn't do, not the things we did do. Let's get out there and take some risks. Playing it safe is an awful waste of the opportunities and chances we are always given.

Emotional Ditches

I had another few wobbles yesterday. The day started well and I travelled for a couple of hours to look at some things. When I returned, I needed to make some decisions and couldn't. It's not the right time to buy, so I must be patient. Indecision can be quite crippling. I'm a great believer in researching the market before taking the plunge, but I'm also a believer in gut instincts and acting quickly when they happen. The trouble arises when the mind ticks off the boxes in a very logical way and we manage to get close to what we want, but there isn't that instant wow factor. Additionally, if someone else is involved in the decision making that just compounds the problem. They've often not invested the same time or energy into the research and just make quick decisions that hurt.

This morning, I have decided to wait. I have made the decision to reassess the situation later in the year and hopefully get something better. The niggles are still there that I might be losing out, but I must put those behind me and move on. I've got to turn my attention to other things and stop any negative thoughts from creeping in. But maybe I'll never find anything like this again. Maybe I have one opportunity and I'm passing this one up. That's when things start to get tricky and that's when there is a danger the depression triggers can kick in.

I'm using buying something as just one example of how we can return to unhelpful thinking patterns in a very short space of time. If we become programmed into regret, we can make our lives a misery. That often happens after a relationship crumbles. We regret its passing and think we may be missing out, particularly, when we wanted it to continue. We think that it was so perfect for us, we will never find anything like it in the rest of our lives. We keep ticking off all the pro boxes about the relationship and forget to tick the cons. We remember those gut feelings of 'this is the one,' 'this is my partner for life' and forget about the seedy side of the relationship at the end. That's what regret does. It blinds us to the cons and backs us into a mental corner. The only way to get out of that corner is to make a decision to move on. There will always be another car, there will always be another house. There will always be another partner.

After a month of depression-free living, I don't want to return to those dark spaces. I must be on the alert for possible sabotage of my mental health. When we feel the wobbles beginning to kick in, we must take positive steps to regain our balance and carry on upright and securely. These little stones that catch the front wheel of our bike and put us off balance can happen at any time. We need to be able to readjust instantly or we'll wobble so much, we'll fall off and end up in an emotional ditch. These emotional ditches are awful. They also contain the emotional debris from every part of our life, so if we accidentally arrive there from some relatively insignificant route, we'll end up wallowing in a quicksand of unrelated emotions that will truly suck us under. One tiny non-relationship regret can lead to a quagmire of relationship regret.

Now, I've got all of this out of my system, I'm ready to move on. There will be other versions of these things to buy in the future and they'll probably be much better. It wasn't meant to be and that's all there is to it. The decision has been made and it is time to move forward with a clear mind and a happy heart. I'm upright again and well away from those emotional ditches. Isn't life amazing?

A Clean House

I cleaned the house yesterday and it felt good. Not the actual cleaning part of it, but the end result. I've done a lot of cleaning over the years and used to spend hours behind a vacuum cleaner in my old house which was quite capacious. These days, it's just a half-hour job, so the results are quicker. Downsizing has been part of my new life post-separation and divorce. Lots of things in my life have changed and they take quite a bit of getting used to.

Change is an ongoing thing in our lives whether we like it or not. Sometimes, it's forced upon us and at other times, it's just a gradual process that's hardly perceptible. The latter is probably more like evolving than changing and is perhaps the more organic of the processes. Sudden change is hard to deal with and when you are a home lover like me, it can be traumatic. I guess it depends a lot on our personalities. I like stability in every aspect of my life, but particularly, in my relationships. It's the whole business of building a nest with the person you love and settling in with your whole future together mapped out. Not like a prison sentence, of course, more like a natural course of events. My parents married quite young and stayed together for their whole lives, I imagined I would be exactly the same when I got married. I believed in the institution of marriage because it represented an undertaking of commitment, through thick and thin and until death us do part.

I never for one moment thought my marriage would ever fail, it was inconceivable to me. It was the constant in my life that I thought was assured forever. I think I've been a very naive person in my life and was probably setting myself up for a big fall when I got married with those high-rolling ideals. But you don't think about that when you're in love and certainly not when you're head-over-heels in love. I was marrying my first love with very little experience of such matters behind me. What an idealistic plonker! How could I have been so stupid? Most of the people around me had countless relationships before they settled on their partner for life, why did I think I could be different? I'm not sure

I can really answer that question as it just seemed the right thing for me to do at the time. I was totally committed and put my heart and soul into winning the girl of my dreams over. It worked.

The fact that the relationship worked for over twenty years probably means it had something going for it and certainly a lot of those years were very happy. But maybe we were both naive to begin with and when my wife lost her naivety, the magic was gone. My naivety remained and continues to this very day. I don't think I'll ever change as it's just the way I am. Despite everything that has happened to me, I think I still believe in the sanctity of marriage. But maybe I shouldn't? Perhaps, I should go by the 'once bitten, twice shy' maxim? Or maybe it's just a matter of finding someone who shares your ideals?

Fortunately, I think I've found someone who does. No relationship is ever perfect and there are always niggles to deal with, but as long as you are both heading in the same direction and share similar ideals, I think we can all remain true to ourselves. We can't change our fundamental principles and remain true to ourselves, it's impossible. I think this is where my marriage went wrong. My wife changed and I stayed the same. It became a recipe for disaster. The change takes place so gradually that it's something that can't be spotted easily. But when it happens—for whatever reason—your ideals are no longer in tune and you cease to resonate together as a couple. Neither of you can remain true to yourselves and the partnership ends. It's heartbreaking, particularly for the person who hasn't changed.

But such is life and we must learn to adapt and roll with the punches. Hopefully, my new life with my new partner will mean that my ideals can remain in place. I can build another safe nest with her and we will both uphold the same shared values. We will be honest, loyal and loving and not tempted by materialistic things. We can be jointly naive and not be ashamed of it. My ex can do whatever she likes and with whomever she likes without ever hurting me again. I like a clean house.

Stuff

When we are basically good-natured, it's easy to forget the harm that our ex has caused us. We take everything on the chin and do our very best to move forward because that's the only way to rebuild our lives. But every now and then, the flashbacks happen and it's time to face up to their cruelty. They ripped the ground from under us and changed the course of our very existence in a very selfish way. If you were like me, you left everything behind because you couldn't face seeing anything that might remind you of them. Treasured possessions that you'd acquired over a long period of time; beautiful objects that were bought with love and care. A lifetime of memories, just gone in a flash. Utterly cruel and selfish. What's more, even if I had managed to have the courage to take other things, my ex would have quibbled over the items and there would have been more unpleasant exchanges. Yet more emotional blackmail and yet more heartache. These people are obnoxious and we are well rid of them. They are basically dishonest and rotten human beings. Mine even reneged on everything she said she would do that wasn't in the Separation Agreement. I made everything so easy for her and she couldn't even do the right thing after that.

Of course, I'm sounding bitter and I realise this doesn't achieve anything. In the great scheme of things, this is only stuff and stuff has no value. People have value. It's important to deal with people with respect. I will probably think about those objects in the future and feel a little bit sad, but I realise I did the best thing I could at the time by making a clean break. Stuff is just stuff and you can always get more stuff, you simply can't put a value on emotional health. I might not be surrounded by beautiful objects or live in a big house or travel the world (even if it were possible these days) but I do have self-respect and peace of mind. I also have a wonderful new partner who understands me and doesn't spend all of her time trying to bully me or undermine everything I say. Life is good, who needs stuff.

I think it is very important that we begin to see the whole picture rather than concentrate on the individual aspects of our failed relationship. As time goes by, we can view the experience with detachment once the hurt has subsided. Even my little outburst above doesn't have the vitriolic punch it used to have. I might be venting my bitterness at certain aspects of the breakup, but overall, it's not going to leave me an emotional wreck for the rest of the day. Likewise, on the occasions my thoughts go back and I don't block them, the stabs in the heart aren't as cutting as they used to be. Maybe I'm on the road to recovery? I hope so.

But maybe it's also that the fight has gone out of me. After two and a half years of energy-draining thoughts, I've had enough. Now, it's a matter of moving forward and looking ahead to a wonderful new life with a wonderful new person. The past has gone and the stuff with it. It's time to furnish my new life with new things and marvel at every new day and be thankful.

Today

Today will be a short entry as I haven't got much time. Suffice it to say, I found myself idly thinking about my ex this morning and I could almost feel myself being dragged back into the old grooves—scary stuff! At least, I had the sense to block those thoughts before they took hold. We must realise when they happen and have the determination to do something about them. I think the problem is that after a month of not allowing this to happen, my guard was down and I didn't think it would do any harm. I imagined I was strong enough to cope. I'm not, we're not, so don't do it.

I think we all have to live with a certain sadness in our hearts about the way things transpired, it's inevitable. I sometimes wonder if my ex ever thinks the same. But I guess for her, she made the decision to leave, so maybe there is just relief. I somehow doubt it though. Deep down there must be some sort of remorse. Anyway, we all need to learn to live with this sadness in one way or another and make the most of the rest of our lives. Every day is a new life since we are not the same person we were yesterday. Time marches on and whether we like it or not, yesterday will never return. Five minutes ago, will not return and that's how precious life is.

Relationships are probably the hardest things we have to deal with in our lives because they are emotionally based. Everything else in life is much more transparent. Houses, cars, jobs and things come and go, but often emotional attachments remain embedded in us for the rest of our lives. We probably need to have an emotional compartment in our minds to put these things into. File them away forever, or maybe only occasionally visit them and see if we can make any sense of them with the passage of time. I think the pain does diminish over time with some memories, but most will always contain some sting. We need to be very selective if we want to remain undamaged.

Today is another new day and although I haven't the time to think about how great it is right now; I know it is and I should be very thankful to be alive. We all should be. Have a great day and I'll be here tomorrow.

On the Same Page

In any relationship, there will always be times when misunderstandings occur—sometimes, it can even be booze-induced, which isn't ideal. These misunderstandings can be deep-seated or just superficial. The superficial ones are easy to deal with because you simply kiss and make up the next day and life goes on as usual. The deep-seated ones are much harder to cope with and can lead to pretty drastic results. Being able to identify which is which is probably one of the most important things to learn in any relationship.

When the lines of communication break down and you stop listening to each other, it is very difficult to find a constructive way forward. Each party repeatedly states their case and neither really listens. It's a stubbornness brought on by a host of different factors. One might be the length of time you've been together; another might be a growing dissatisfaction with what the other person is saying. Whatever the root cause, the result is the same, an ever-widening gap in that personal bond that unites two people and keeps them together.

Maybe a period of space is a good idea and that's where trial separations come into play. Providing both parties are still faithful to the relationship, this might be very beneficial. Unfortunately, in my case, my wife asked for a trial separation just to see if her new man would work out. Now that stinks. But in genuine cases, where there aren't any external influences involved—and these could sadly be destructive and meddling friends—each party has the opportunity to re-assess things and hopefully come to think about and value the partnership that has often lasted the test of time. It's much better to do such a reassessment when the relationship still has the possibility of continuing, rather than leaving it to a time when there is no going back.

It's quite bizarre writing about all these things when my own relationship went pear-shaped, but I do it in the hope that I can help in some way by talking it through. It is all obvious stuff, but sometimes, we just miss the obvious and plough on regardless. We miss the obvious signs that things are not what they

92

used to be. We miss the signs that cracks are appearing in that special bond that keeps people together. We miss the signs that our other half might be looking elsewhere for love because we've forgotten how to furnish it. It's very sad.

I think today's entry is directed at people who are on the cusp of things going pear-shaped and trying to work out what to do. It is also aimed at myself as a warning never to let things get out of hand ever again. See the signs and do something about it. Better still, don't let the signs develop at all. What I think I'm trying to say is, don't give up on a relationship without making every effort to make it work. Try to find some common ground and discuss things sensibly. Make some space to think and see things objectively. It is a lot to throw away if you don't. The emotional pain is excruciating post-breakup and if it's avoidable, try to avoid it.

But it always takes both parties to be on the same page and that's the tricky bit. Finding a way to get back on the same page is the challenge, but one that is really worth fighting for.

Mars and Venus

Today, I want to talk about the difference between the male and the female perspective in relationship issues. Of course, being male, I am no expert on the female side of things, so this will be completely one-sided. But I think there definitely is a difference because of our biological makeup and how we are programmed to survive as a species.

Women are programmed to bring up children and they have a single-mindedness in this approach that makes them amazingly strong. Even when they don't have children, that single-mindedness is still there. Part of this desire to protect and nurture their children involves cooperation with other mothers who also have the same instincts. To stay strong, they forge relationships outside the one with their partner and this generally leaves them in a much better position to cope with a breakup. We hunter-gatherer guys are a lot less social and although we might cooperate to bring home the bacon, we seldom spend much time talking about nurturing and child-rearing. We are quite happy talking about such things with our partners but seldom indulge in lengthy conversations with our buddies. We don't have the same single-mindedness about protecting our offspring either, preferring to let them learn by experience rather than rushing to bail them out at the slightest danger.

This doesn't make us insensitive; it just seems to make us more aloof emotionally. But deep down, without the strong female mothering survival instinct, we are actually quite weak emotionally. It doesn't take much for us to be emotional wrecks—and I can talk from personal experience on this score. This female ability to focus on their offspring also gives them the ability to focus on themselves even without offspring. It's a kind of survival instinct by association. If they survive, maybe their future offspring have a better chance of surviving. It might also have a bearing on whom they choose as fathers of their children. Much better strong and successful rather than weak and ineffectual.

As men, we admire this emotional strength and try to tap into it. We become reliant on our partners to look after our emotional needs. When they decide to leave us, all of that emotional support disappears and that's when the trouble starts. We are completely lost and devoid of any sense of emotional direction in life. We also can't imagine how on earth anyone could be so cruel as to abandon us in such a heartless fashion. Our ex becomes this cold monster who we just don't understand. We have been abandoned by our substitute mums. We're all little boys desperate to be looked after for the rest of our lives.

It's a sad picture to paint, but there is a lot of truth in it. The statistics indicate that it takes men a hell of a lot longer to get over a relationship breakup. We need to rebuild our emotional strength and the only way we can do this is to find another partner who can satisfy these needs. Everyone needs emotional stability, but I think men need it far more than is generally thought. Fortunately, there is a growing awareness that this is an area that needs to be addressed. With a bit of luck, men will also have support networks in the future and those desperate periods of loneliness will be a thing of the past.

Mediation

Resentment is a killer; it creeps up on us and devours us like Necrotising Fasciitis. It eats away at us on a daily basis until there is nothing left but a skeleton. It's the root cause of so many relationship failures. It seems to occur when one party believes they have contributed to the relationship more than the other. It becomes a deep-seated niggle that just won't go away. In some cases, these gripes are quite real and unless addressed, the relationship will struggle. But in many cases, both parties feel they have genuine grounds to think the balance of power is not quite right.

This sort of impasse is difficult to overcome without some clear negotiations. But often negotiating becomes impossible because both parties are not listening to each other—particularly, in a long-term relationship, they think they have heard it all before, so what's the point? The trouble with this attitude is that it leads nowhere. It's a stubbornness on both sides that just continues the status quo. The resentments remain and the flesh-eating disease just gets worse.

In this situation, I think the only sensible answer is to seek independent advice. Joint counselling sessions give both parties the opportunity to air their grievances in a neutral environment. Each person can tell their side of the story and the independent counsellor can make an objective assessment and try to find some common ground. Unfortunately, in my case, my ex refused to go to counselling because she'd already decided the relationship was over long before I knew anything about it. When that happens, there is little hope for a resolution and probably little hope for the relationship.

Resentment is also often brought on by jealousy. One partner sees the other living a perfect life at their expense. They have managed to stack all the cards in their favour and are oblivious to the other person's needs. This is another area that is difficult to deal with without mediation, particularly, if the one who is happy can't see where the problem lies. When we get jealous, there is only a finite amount of time we can deal with it before it becomes a major issue. The other person needs to understand that the relationship can't move forward if they remain stubborn and self-righteous. They need to be made aware by someone independent that they must make certain allowances. If one party refuses to consider counselling, they have obviously made up their mind that they are right and don't want anyone to change that decision. Now, that's a recipe for the end.

No Pain, No Gain?

Yesterday, I found myself offering advice on relationship matters, rather than reflecting on my own experiences which have been the main purpose of this diary. It's a very tricky area to get involved in because everyone has a different set of circumstances and a totally different set of priorities. I know that the people I valued most were those who gave me unconditional love and support without trying to tell me what, or what not to do. The few mutual friends I've retained still keep in touch to see how I'm getting on, not to find out any juicy bits of gossip or to update me on how my ex is getting along. They are to be treasured.

The trouble is, when you've been through what I've been through in the last few years, you desperately want to help anyone else who faces the same challenges. You want to try and make things better for them, or even help them avoid going through the whole damn thing if that's at all possible. But there doesn't seem to be any relationship handbook that we can all consult and come out of things unscathed. It's as if the pain is an integral part of the healing process and, to quote a well-worn phrase, *no pain, no gain*. But I do think, it is important to have someone to talk to when the shit hits the fan. For us guys, our confidant has gone and we need to find someone else who will listen. They might not be able to help in any tangible way, but they allow us to air our thoughts and by doing so, try to make sense of what seems to be a hopeless situation. I was very fortunate to have my brother with me when my marriage fell apart and he became my sounding board for the first month of this hellish journey. It can't have been easy for him as I poured out everything. The anger, the grief, the feelings of betrayal…everything. I'll never be able to thank him enough for that. After that, I had further support from more distant family members who gave me space to try and find myself again. I walked for at least two hours every day, pounding the pavements and beaches with a sense of purpose, but not quite knowing what it was because my life was so empty without my ex. There was a desperate loneliness in my heart even with such love and support around me. But having that love and support around me was vital, even if ultimately, no one could solve this problem for me.

In a way, we aren't really open to advice when all those emotions are whirring around. We know deep down that our problems can't be solved by anyone else. The person closest to us has let us down and left us to flounder and we must somehow find a way to pick ourselves up and move on. In the heat of this abandonment, it is also very difficult to be objective and try to understand why we were dumped. At such a low-ebb in our lives, it's probably not a good idea to explore those feeling either. Blaming ourselves for a situation that was ultimately beyond our control is useless and just leads to more pain. In my case, the damage was done, my wife had moved on both physically and emotionally and her mind was made up way before I could do anything about it. With hindsight—and two and a half years later—maybe I should have handled things differently. But quite honestly, I was a different person then and was unable to make sense of anything that was going on. I was devoted to my wife and thought we would be together forever. Even when things got strained, deep down I couldn't contemplate life without her, she was almost part of my DNA.

However, that was then and this is now. I am a totally different person and no doubt the enormous amount of pain and heartache that I have been through has been a tremendous learning curve. Would I want to go through it again? NEVER. It has been the most painful time in my life and an experience I wouldn't wish on anyone. It's been absolute hell and nearly finished me off. It has taught me a number of things though and changed my perspective on life. I think I said in a previous entry that maybe my ex did me a favour by forcing the issue because if she hadn't, I certainly wouldn't. But I've also acknowledged that she changed in our relationship and I didn't, so we couldn't head along the same path anymore. If you are not heading together in a similar direction with the same hopes and dreams, it's very difficult to continue to click. But some couples manage to reignite their relationship throughout their marriage and I can't help but admire them.

As for me, I think I'm out of the desert and finding my way at last, and even if I have to face further problems in my life, I will at least be able to cope a bit better. My journey has been a long and very painful one, but I couldn't have made it without those wonderful people who kept on loving me regardless. They allowed me to start loving myself again when I thought I was just worthless. What more could I ask for?

Enjoy the Surprises

Today, I want to focus on positive things and reassure everyone (and myself) that there is life after a failed relationship. When I was going through my 'no pain, no gain' period, I found that thought almost impossible to comprehend. Everything was doom and gloom and the world seemed like a very dark place to inhabit. But now that the sun is beginning to peek through again, there is a realisation that no matter how much shit is thrown at us, eventually, we'll find a way to move forward.

For me, this transformation came together in a number of different ways. Firstly, when I realised there was no going back to my marriage, I concentrated on finding a new partner who could restore my faith in womankind. Despite everything, I still retained the belief that not all women were heartless creatures capable of anything. My instincts told me that if I tried hard enough, there would be someone out there with similar core beliefs and morals as my own. After such a rough time with my ex, I'm not sure where this belief came from, but it was there nonetheless. Following a relatively unsuccessful foray into online dating that lasted about two months and only produced two dinner dates, I finally struck lucky and met my present partner. She is in the same profession and has the same outlook on life.

I've been very lucky, since not every new partner would be prepared to handle all the emotional baggage that came with me. As I was dumped and didn't do the dumping, I was still very much emotionally tied up with my ex—after 24 years together, that's hardly surprising. I was grieving for my marriage in a big way despite all the betrayal and dishonesty. I needed to move forward but couldn't let the past go. Fortunately, my new partner was mature enough to realise that this was a stage I needed to go through and she supported me in a very selfless way. She had her own baggage, of course (don't we all), so there were mutual adjustments to be made, but we made them. In just over two years, we have discovered a lot about each other and my partner's faith in me I hope is reaping rewards. My life is so much less stressful and we try to maintain a life of mutual admiration, not conflict.

The second element of my transformation really comes out of the first. In order to truly make my new relationship work, I needed to let go of the past. This was probably the hardest thing to do and an area I still occasionally struggle with, although in the last month, I've managed remarkably well mainly due to this diary. I've continually used the blocking techniques I've talked about in the past, so that now even the slightest wandering memory is blocked instantly and can't take hold. I've done this so often, the neural pathways are disappearing. This really has helped me stave off depression. However, it really needs to become a habit and the slightest weakness in this respect can be disastrous. Whenever a thought appears in my mind that might lead down the depression highway, I block it immediately and think of something else. For me, it's the only way to stay mentally healthy.

The third element in my transformation involves viewing life flexibly. I have taken a more relaxed approach to everything. What will be, will be, has become something of a motto for me. After all, I've survived the biggest challenge in my life and I'm still alive. More than that, I'm actually beginning to enjoy life again. All the fretting and anxiety in the world doesn't help you and just drags you into a still further dark place. If we can have the confidence to know that we can deal with whatever comes our way, we won't worry about it. Life will be good. The unpredictability of life is part of its charm. Enjoy the surprises!

Life's Precious Gift

I didn't sleep well last night and caught myself tempted to think about the past. There seem to be quite a few blips in this recovery process and just when you think you have life sussed, a moment of weakness sets in and you are off down the highway to hell once again. But luckily, I avoided any major slide backwards. As soon as the thoughts began to spring into my head and I could feel a wave of panic come over me, I thought about something else. It's a weird feeling when the thoughts come back again; your whole body becomes flushed with regret. It's something that happened every day for years, so I know the warning signs well. I used to allow one thought to follow on from another and the results were pretty dire.

I think in coming to terms with the regret, we need to come to terms with our often-dramatic change of life. All the things we did with our ex have disappeared, so there is a gaping hole there. Even if we share the same activities with our new partner, it can never be the same. We regret the passing of some magical moments in our lives and that can be painful. But what we must remind ourselves is that most of those memories are idealised and it's dangerous to give them too much weight. For me, if I start to go down that path, one idealised memory leads to another and soon I'm feeling very depressed. I start to remember the hopes and dreams we once shared together and the amazing conversations we had around them. I can't recall actual moments, but the feelings tend to come back if I let them. It's so tempting to indulge in these sorts of recollections but also so dangerous for our mental health.

I know I'm tending to go round and round in circles with this diary, but that's all part of the process. I need to reinforce in my mind what my priorities are. I need to eliminate the triggers that lead to depression. If that involves changing my dreams or at the very least adjusting them, so be it. If I'm hell-bent on pursuing the same dreams that I had with my ex, that's probably foolhardy. I'll need to modify them for my new relationship and not get sucked into the old thought patterns that are done and dusted. I think living a day at a time is one way to get back on track. Enjoy the now rather than putting off the enjoyment to some later date that may or may not come. So often we spend so much time in the past and planning for an idealised future that we forget to make the most of the here and now. We forget to savour the joys of this moment, no matter how simple they may be. I have been all over the world and visited some amazing places, but those memories shouldn't dominate the rest of my life, even if I was brave enough to recall them at the moment. When I'm stronger—maybe in a few years' time—I hope I'll be able to dip into them without getting upset. What matters is now and how happy I am at the moment. Life is full of contrasts and we should enjoy that. Life is full of different experiences and some might be humdrum and some might be exciting, but they should all be celebrated regardless. What matters is peace of mind and that all-too-important elimination of internal chatter. Ok, I could be in St Mark's Square in Venice now rather than writing this diary. But how much happier would I really be? It could be stinking hot there and I might have been charged 10 Euros for a coffee. I might be with someone who is moaning about the trip or forcing me to do something when all I want to do is sit down and have a long lunch with a bottle of wine. At least while writing this diary, I'm feeling content and not hassled by anyone. I'm not being forced into anyone else's expectations. Continuously striving for the impossible. Maybe a bucket list of visiting every conceivable place on the earth. These sorts of expectations become burdens after a while and the whole experience becomes a chore.

I'm glad I have experienced what I have, but I was always more interested in observing people and cultures rather than ticking off the tourist attractions. I could never understand what the point was in photographing something that had been photographed a million times before. Even now, I sometimes get sucked into the 'I've been there too' game. It usually happens at dinner parties and involves people who are asserting how upwardly mobile they are. I think I'm over all of that. At one time, I'd jump in and be keen to show off how well travelled I am, but not now. The small things in life are more important and being content just to sit in the same room with your partner and do your own thing is just as rewarding as racing around the world trying to tick off boxes. Maybe I've modified my expectations because of necessity, but who cares, the main thing is that I'm not stressed out trying to live a life keeping up with the Joneses.

Perhaps, some people would view this change of focus as a copout, but for me, it is just a growing realisation that competing is not a way to live. In the end, you even end up competing with the people closest to you and that's a recipe for disaster. The simple contentment in your relationship is lost in favour of greed and ambition. You both start to think that the only important thing in life is winning. You forget that the only really important thing in life is loving and being loved. You can love and be loved watching a movie snuggled up in bed. In fact, it's often easier in that setting than in a crowded St Mark's Square. Maybe we should always concentrate on the simple and fundamental things in life first, before letting our egos get out of hand. We mustn't let the glitz and the glamour and the money and the pretend lifestyle cloud what matters most. Life's really precious gifts are the simplest things imaginable, if we could only but see them.

Acceptance (2)

Last night, I dreamt about my ex again, but only in passing. I was talking to someone I was booking a room with and mentioned that I had been married for a long time but it had ended a number of years ago. It's probably a subconscious sign that I am finally accepting it's all over and moving on. It's taken a very long time to get to this point and the journey has been a long and gruelling one, but I'm glad I'm here. Acceptance is a really important thing to achieve and the only way to move forward.

It's not only accepting that my ex may as well be dead to me, but it's also accepting that my life has changed dramatically and I need to re-evaluate my priorities. Yesterday, I pointed to the need to love and be loved and I think this is paramount to any happy life. It provides emotional stability that allows us to contemplate almost anything. If we are in this kind of loving relationship that is not judgemental but accepting, we have the freedom to take risks, because risks sometimes lead to failure. Failure is an important part of life and one of our most important learning tools. In my previous relationship, failure was always seen as a sign of weakness. My ex-wife couldn't accept it in herself or anyone around her, so it made the very act of loving someone extremely difficult for her because no one is perfect and least of all me.

I was thinking about this point last night as I cooked dinner. I decided to modify a recipe and do my own take on it. My ex would never do this, always sticking to the steps very precisely. She would get very upset if things went wrong, particularly, if I had anything to do with it. Cooking for a dinner party often became a very stressful occasion because she wanted to be seen to be perfect, even more so when her mother was one of the guests. She had grown up in an environment where success was rewarded and failure derided. It led to a very tense human condition. I always tried to ameliorate the situation by making light of everything and saying that it didn't matter, but that made me flippant and uncaring. Don't get me wrong, my ex-wife's perfectionism often led to amazing results both in the culinary department and in other aspects of her life, but it also left her less able to deal with my obvious foibles. At the start of our marriage, she was a lot more open as this new-found freedom with me was such a refreshing change from her parents' approach. In fact, I'm sure I took the pressure off during the whole of her university days and well into her career. However, the more confident she became, the less she needed my casual approach to life and the need to be seen to be perfect became an overarching goal. Success and winning became her raison d'être.

My new partner is a completely different person. She doesn't care if my experiments fail in just the same way that I don't care if her experiments fail. We have a chuckle together and don't give it a second thought. Often, our experiments actually produce some really interesting results that are very tasty and with a slight modification, become part of our staple fare. But we are like that in every aspect of our lives together. We accept each other's foibles and don't make an issue out of them. In this loving atmosphere, life is so stressless and calm. I'm sure it's the way life should be. Of course, there will always be times when we agree to disagree over an approach, but we still *agree* to disagree. There will also be times when external relationships sometimes come between us, but we always try to compromise and keep things working.

In the end, we have to be accepting of many things in order to make a relationship work. But that's the nature of loving and being loved. If we love someone, we actually accept them for who they are, warts and all. When the chemistry is really right, we don't even notice their foibles, because love is blind and that's the way it should be.

Humanity

Yesterday, I talked about the human need to love and be loved and this permeates our whole life. In its simplest form, it's the love we give and receive from our family, in its broadest form it's reciprocal love for humanity as a whole. We can't go through life without influencing and being influenced by other people and often this is just a different form of love.

In order to make any interaction with other people work we must find some common ground. We need to be on the same page intellectually and emotionally. We need to share common values and be striving for similar things in life. These are the building blocks of friendship. It takes years to add to these blocks and make friendships that last a lifetime, just as it takes years to form loving relationships that last. In the early stages, it's often a case of two steps forward and one step back as we test the water. But over time, we gain confidence in each other and despite the minor setbacks, our bond grows stronger and stronger. That's being in love in its broadest sense and this could be the love of a partner or a friend.

I think my failed relationship has taught me a lot of things, but primarily, it's taught me not to take anything in life for granted. I was far too complacent about my marriage and thought it was indestructible. I thought that as long as I stayed faithful to my wife and tried to do whatever she wanted, everything would be ok. That wasn't enough and I paid the price. I realise now that every day should be a new start to the relationship and we should be just as interested in our partners now as we were on the first day we met. I mustn't blame myself for what happened because in the end, my ex treated me abominably, but I must also acknowledge that I should have tried harder. My ex needed more from me and I obviously wasn't in a position to give more for a whole host of reasons.

Everything in life is about renewal and it will be until the day we die. It's so easy to become complacent and stop making the effort to renew ourselves because this is actually the spice of life. We all have the ability to be different people today than we were yesterday. We have this ability if we just make the effort. I should have made the effort in my marriage and my wife should have done the same thing. But what is done is done and the important thing for me is to learn from the experience. Ultimately, it isn't anyone's fault, because we are all just learning. We are learning from the day we are born until the day we die. We take two steps forward and one step back all the way through our lives. The important thing is to only take one step back; in that way, we'll be making some sort of headway.

I've been through hell learning these simple truths, but at least I've been learning. Let's just promise ourselves that we will be better people tomorrow than we were today. Let's learn something about ourselves today so that the new person that wakes up and lives, breathes and has fun tomorrow, is a better person. If we do that, we'll be making the very best contribution to humanity in all its different guises.

You Can't Afford the Luxury
of a Negative Thought

It is now 46 days since I started this diary and I haven't experienced any major periods of depression. There have been the odd moments where if I had continued on a certain line of thought I would have been dragged back into the same dark places that I have inhabited for over two and a half years. This is a major breakthrough for me and one that I am determined to continue, come what may. Depression is awful and probably one of the world's biggest killers.

You can rid yourself of depression too if you can only consistently block out the negative thoughts, but it requires practice and consistency. In one of my sleepless moments last night, I thought about this a good deal. By the way, these sleepless times used to be filled with negative thoughts that went into endless depressive cycles. These days, I'm happy to use them constructively, in fact, I think of them constructively. Anyway, I know this is a bit of a far-fetched analogy, but I started to think about cleaning the shower and bath. I've done this sort of cleaning a lot over the years as it wasn't something my ex considered to be her role in life—far too self-important for such menial jobs. In my bathroom cleaning role, I soon realised that if you did nothing, although things looked ok on the surface, when you eventually did take to using a detergent you'd find a huge scum had accumulated without you even noticing it. It was disgusting and very, very hard to get rid of. Over a period of time, I realised that if I got into the habit of spraying the whole shower cubicle and the bath after every couple of uses and left the detergent to do its thing overnight, all I needed to do was rinse it off and it kept things beautifully clean. No scrubbing and no disgusting scum.

We need to avoid the mental scum that accumulates without us even noticing it. This is where a daily habit is so important, not only a daily habit, but an every-moment-of-the-day habit. As soon as a negative thought comes into your mind-BLOCK IT. Think of something else or replace it with a good image you have stored away for that very purpose. I've talked about this in a lot of detail in my earlier diary entries and it works. My brother recently commented on how women seem to be able to switch off and get on with their lives while we blokes simply stew over things endlessly. So true, so why the hell don't we take a leaf out of their book and do exactly the same thing? It's not rocket science and that's precisely what I have been learning over the last 40-odd days. Block out the negative thoughts and just get on with your life. It works and I am living proof of it.

Men are always trying to fix things. We want to know how things work and if they break down, we want to fix them. But this leads to all sorts of complications when we are trying to 'fix' emotional problems because we can't fix them because so often there isn't any logical explanation as to why they broke down in the first place. It's a hiding to nothing. No, it's just a hiding to hell. I tried to understand what had gone wrong with my marriage by going over things endlessly in my mind. I couldn't understand why my wife had moved on without giving me the opportunity to fix things. I couldn't understand that after 24 years together, you wouldn't want to try to fix things. But women are more pragmatic. Of course, if the car won't start on Monday, they'll let the battery recover overnight and try again on Tuesday. If it still won't work, they may even try again on Wednesday and Thursday or even a handful might plug in the battery charger. Very few will be bothered to give it a second thought as to why it's not working. The simplest thing to do is get another car. My ex wasn't interested in finding out the root cause of our marriage breakdown, since in her own mind, she'd been trying to jump-start it for years. A new model of me came along at just the right time. It started every time, had heaps of extras and was ten years younger. For her, no-brainer or what?

So why on earth did I spend the next two and a half years crucifying myself trying to work out what I should have done to fix things? I'm a bloody idiot, that's why. Well, I was. Emotional things are almost impossible to fix without time…a lot of time. Meanwhile, we can be leading perfectly happy lives just like our exes. Don't go around in a circle trying to fix emotional things that can't be fixed without time. Block out all of those negative thoughts and get on with your life. That's why women can move on from a failed relationship much more quickly than men. It probably isn't because they are inherently cruel or unkind, it's probably just because they have this ability to bury things and move on. They can block the negative thoughts and not revisit them in any shape or form. Whilst we poor sods are wallowing in self-pity trying to make sense of things and fix them, they are living perfectly normal day-to-day lives without a care in the world. WE NEED TO DO THE SAME THING.

When I was going through hell after my ex moved out to spend time with her new man and I couldn't sleep and was desperately depressed, I remember her advising me to just go to the doctor and go on sleeping pills and antidepressants. She wasn't the least bit interested in trying to 'fix' the fundamental problem which was my devastation and heartbreak. This was characteristic of that whole pre-separation time. She could bury all of her feelings in a single-minded determination to move on. It didn't matter how much her lies and deceit hurt me and it didn't matter what sort of pain she was inflicting on me; the end justified the means and she could bury everything. She texted her lover openly and just lied when I challenged her. She even phoned him and when I overheard the conversation, she lied about who it was. It was an absolutely despicable way to treat someone you supposedly once loved. But by then, of course, it really was a case of 'once loved.' The love had gone or at the very least, the love that had been there was well and truly blocked out.

The textbook answer to any relationship breakup is to keep busy and find a distraction. Well, having gone through what I have, I couldn't agree more. The only problem with this excellent advice is that we guys just can't get into that mindset quickly enough. We are always too busy beating ourselves up trying to fix things. DON'T. Block out the negative thoughts and let the emotional things sort themselves out over time. By blocking out the negative thoughts that lead to spiralling depression, you'll have the ability to think about other things and enjoy the distractions. You'll be able to get on with your life. Please, please, don't give those negative thoughts the time of day. Get rid of them as soon as one pops into your head. If you don't, you'll spiral back to the same dark place every single time. I've said this before and I'll say it again: You can't afford the luxury of a negative thought.

Beware of the Subconscious Can of Worms

Well, so much for my wonderful solution to my conscious problems! Last night, I dreamt about my ex again and got a bit depressed in my dream, which made me a bit depressed when I woke up. I know what triggered this and it was a conscious glimpse of her yesterday in one of those mobile phone memory photos that crop up from time to time. Unfortunately, my blocking techniques are not sophisticated enough to work when I'm asleep. Bugger! Quite a bit of this dream concerned my former house which I loved and the regret of losing it. She was there too of course but had just swanned into my dream to gloat. Yep, a rather sad dream of regret.

But I'm awake now and mustn't dwell on the dream too much as this could lead to all manner of depressing thoughts. I sometimes think my subconscious mind is helping me, but at other times, it seems to be playing devil's advocate. Weird or what? It does make me think do I really know myself? Probably not. Life is a matter of self-discovery from the day we are born until the day we die. Even when we consciously try to tame this wild beast called the mind, it tricks us and gives us a side-swipe that we can't avoid. It's kind of funny having a battle with yourself! For the last month, I've been wrestling with the negative chatter from within and not letting it get hold of me. It's been a conscious effort to eliminate the negative and accentuate the positive and it's working. Dreams like that are just dirty, backdoor tactics and I'm not impressed. The good thing is that I can joke about it and not let it spoil my day, or destroy all the good work I've done so far.

Maybe we are actually made up of multiple personalities and they are always vying for dominance. If we let the negative ones take hold, we become angry, resentful and unpleasant. If we let the positive ones take hold, we are kind, generous and optimistic. I certainly know which ones I want to have in the driving seat. That's the whole point of this writing experiment, I want the good personalities to prevail and I want to bury those other monster personalities that dwell within me. It's the constant battle between good and evil that pervades our lives and dominates our society. I say multiple personalities because each comes in a different guise. The angry one is obvious, although I'm not too familiar with him, thank goodness. Then there is the spiteful one who holds grudges and always wants revenge. But perhaps the worst is the glass-half-empty personality who wants to put a damper on everything. It's always looking for ways to drag you down, make you overly cautious and stop you from enjoying life. That one is the personification of negativity and I want shot of it.

The truth is, we can't have one without the other, because life is a matter of contrasts and we need to accept that. What is really important is getting the balance right and not letting the destructive side take over. Awareness is the key. In everyday life, we will meet people who err on the negative spectrum and drag us into their dark world. If we associate with them too much, their negative tendencies will rub off on us. Our whole society is geared towards the negative; most news is not good news, but negative news. We are bombarded by stories of destruction and chaos and it sinks in by osmosis. I think as long as we are aware of this, we can avoid it. I tend to turn off the TV or radio news for that very reason. The presenters seem to have an evil delight in headlining the latest list of disasters and conflicts. They can't wait to get hold of a juicy negative story that they can repeat ad infinitum—it's bordering on the sick. We need to steer clear of these doom-and-gloom mongers when they appear collectively or singly.

This entry started out by trying to identify the evils within us but quickly turned to those outside. This is simply because they have a symbiotic relationship; one is dependent on the other. We are what we consume. If we consume a heap of negative garbage, we'll fuel the negative sides of our personalities and become depressed and a naysayer. If we associate with negative people, we'll become like them. Over long periods of time, this negativity just seeps in without us even knowing about it. The visual triggers from garbage TV can be very invasive and destructive and easily change our mood. We must be very careful about what goes in. The old saying garbage in, garbage out is so true.

This is a rather long and convoluted way of saying I better watch out for those memory photos on my phone; they can open a subconscious can of worms if I'm not too careful.

Snuffing out Emotional Embers

The focus of this diary has shifted quite a bit from getting over relationship problems to getting over depression and what is broadly termed mental health issues. I'm not sure if there really is a dividing line between depression and mental illness, but for me, the former sounds a lot less scary than the latter. Whatever the terminology, I'm comfortable taking this sidestep because much of the heartache we experience in a relationship failure actually involves quite a bit of depression and its associated states of mind.

On this, the 48th day of my diary, I can confidently say that it is possible to conquer depression and keep yourself away from those dark places if you really try. After two and a half years of utter hell trying to come to terms with the loss of my marriage, I made the decision to start blocking out every negative thought that entered my mind associated with this loss. Whenever an image of my ex appeared in my mind, or I was reminded of her in everyday life, I blocked all of those thoughts in a very deliberate way. I refused to let myself be dragged down those well-worn pathways that I'd created over a period of 30 months. During this time, just one tiny little thought about my ex was enough to send me on a destructive journey every single time. I would revisit the same material over and over again and only ever achieve the same result: deep depression. You see, thinking about the same things over and over again didn't change anything. In fact, the phrase attributed (probably erroneously) to Albert Einstein comes to mind: *The definition of insanity is doing the same thing over and over again and expecting a different result*. But that's what depression does to us, it drags us into a never-ending cycle of negative thoughts.

Relationship breakdowns produce emotional trauma and emotional trauma leads to depression. It's as simple as that. When we are at our lowest ebb, we aren't capable of looking at things objectively, so we take the easiest course which is repetitive and destructive cycles. We think about the same things, we drink too much and we generally forget to look after ourselves physically. We

114

become emotional zombies with little or no direction in life. Ultimately, we've got to get off the treadmill and break all the cycles. Blocking out those thoughts that trigger the thinking cycles is the first place to start because you can't hope to find the motivation to get rid of the others when your overall mood is low. Having said that, a two-pronged approach is probably highly beneficial. Block out the negative thoughts and do a lot of exercise and eat well and cut out some of the excessive grog. Actually, that sounds like more than a two-pronged approach, but what the hell. Lifting yourself from depression is easier if you can use all sorts of different methods.

It's an ongoing regime. I may have successfully negotiated 48 depression-free days but there have been periods where I thought my resolve was weakening. While I was mowing the lawn yesterday, I caught myself thinking about my former life and those tell-tale signs began to come over me. It's awful and I pulled myself together very quickly and thought about something else. I still get those sick feelings that flush through my whole body, but they are now red alert signs for me. I'm sure I'll get them for the rest of my life. It happens with periods of acute embarrassment. If you think back to a moment in your life when you felt utterly ashamed of your actions, you can relive that moment of mortification in an instant. It's that red-faced flush of embarrassment we've all experienced in life. With me, it happens with thoughts of regret and loss as well. I'll just have to live with it. But these moments will be much less painful if I don't follow through with them.

To be honest, I sometimes wonder if I have the strength to keep up the good work. Particularly, when I'm tired, I tend to feel a bit sorry for myself and let my guard down. It's a natural human condition. However, I do know that the longer I don't give in to these evil thoughts, the better chance I have of suppressing them on a regular basis. Indeed, stopping them from appearing altogether. Think back to some really painful times in your life that happened years and years ago. Chances are those painful memories have been well and truly buried. They only appear if we choose to dig them up, they don't otherwise pop up on a regular basis. But even if we choose to exhume them, we can generally deal with them in a more detached and pragmatic way. This is the point we need to be at with our failed relationship issues and we can only get there if we block the emotional triggers and refuse to reinforce those destructive emotional channels.

It might seem that this diary is the antithesis of what I'm recommending since I'm often raking over aspects of my own failed relationship on a daily basis. But the difference is that I'm not responding or indulging in any *emotional* triggers. When I discuss an aspect of my failed relationship, I am discussing it objectively, not emotionally. None of this is emotionally charged. Maybe when I first started writing this diary, emotion played its part and you can see it in the vitriolic language I used, but now everything is calmer and much more controlled. The volcano has erupted and spewed its stuff and all that's left are a few flaming embers dotted around the base. Every time one of those emotional embers flares up, I snuff it out and bury it. Soon the whole damned thing will be dormant and my wonderful new partner and I will be able to go and have a picnic on its beautiful grassy slopes. I can't wait.

Warts and All

I have an early start this morning, so I actually wrote the entry that follows yesterday afternoon. It was a little bit strange writing two entries in one day, but I was determined to keep my writing habit going.

I felt a trifle down this morning but was glad I completed my diary as it concentrated my mind and set me up for the rest of the day. Sometimes, it's difficult to get the creative juices flowing and as I usually have no idea what I'm going to write about, I just have to get started and see where the ideas take me. It's also important not to be too picky. Normally, if I'm writing something really important like a reference for someone or a report, I'll draft it and then spend days revising it. Coming back to it each day with new eyes usually makes it flow better and often irons out any really clunky sentences. Diaries are quite a different kettle of fish and without the luxury of endless revisions, you just have to get them completed warts and all. But I don't care about that, as there are more things to life than trying to seek perfection. Besides, perfection doesn't exist and what we might think of as today's rubbish, we might actually think is quite good tomorrow. Writing quickly also gets the ideas down before we have a chance to muck about with them too much.

I like the idea of things not being too refined, in just the same way that I like hearty food rather than some of the over-complicated cuisine that appeals to the senses rather than to the belly. Not all the time of course, because a well-constructed degustation menu is hard to beat, but a good deal of the time. I could eat pasta and fish until the cows come home. So, what on earth could this have to do with failed relationships, or for that matter combatting depression? I think the keyword is 'refined.' If we start to overthink things in a silly attempt to construct a 'perfect' life, we'll be in for a rude awakening. There is no such thing as a perfect life or a perfect relationship. We are all basically flawed individuals who have to make do with whatever we've been given in life. We shouldn't be afraid of our authentic selves and we shouldn't try to make ourselves into something we aren't. Sadly, when a relationship fails, it's mainly because one member of the partnership isn't happy with the other. They try desperately to change their other half, and in the process, they forget their estimable qualities. They forget what wonderful core beliefs they might have and what amazingly compassionate human beings they might be. They are so keen to live with this perfect human they've created in their minds, they chuck away everything they held dear for so many years. It's tragic and seldom necessary.

I'm not interested in perfection because it's meaningless in art and destructive in human relationships. It's clinical and not in the least bit human. The only people who don't have any problems in the world are buried in the cemetery. Perfection is not existing. So, I sure as hell want to be imperfect. This is just another way of saying we take the good with the bad in any area of our lives. We learn to love our partners' foibles and certainly don't seek to change what is inherently part of them. We see the bigger picture and not the brush strokes. We love our partners holistically and they should love us in exactly the same way.

Instead of trying to change our partner's little annoying habits, why not celebrate them, because they are part of who they are? Don't let's pick holes in them, let's love them warts and all.

Betrayal

I want to talk about betrayal today for a number of reasons. Firstly, I am back in an area where my ex and I spent a lot of time, so the memories associated with this place are still very strong even a few years after we went our separate ways. Secondly, I've been trying to reconcile the act of betrayal in my diary recently in an attempt to be fair and balanced, now that I'm managing to get to grips with the fallout from the end of my marriage.

It's really the aura of this place rather than specific memories that are taking their toll. You share so much over a long period of time, and with time, comes trust. You put an enormous amount of energy into the relationship and care about every aspect of it. For me, it was the most important thing in my life. When my former wife slid on my wedding ring at the ceremony all those years ago, it never left my finger until the day she said there was no going back. It was there for almost 20 years. It was the symbol of the most precious aspect of my life: my wife and my marriage. Call me old fashioned, but I actually believed in 'until death do us part.' There wasn't a bone in my body that thought otherwise. It was simply an act of utter devotion and total commitment and nothing could ever have tempted me to betray her.

I honestly believed that we shared the same faith in each other and that nothing could ever come between us. Of course, there were niggles on the way and every marriage has them, but gaping holes or unassailable difficulties? No way. You think you know someone so well that everything about them is transparent. You know them so well that you can tell when they are fibbing and they can tell when you are fibbing. And fibbing is the worst it ever is, lying to one another would be unthinkable because the bond you share is based on total trust and transparency. That is the sort of marriage I thought I had.

But I was wrong, painfully wrong, and I faced the biggest challenge in my life: Betrayal. This explanation of the word really sums it up: 'The act of someone violating your trust in them...A spouse is betrayed when their partner has an affair. Betrayal is when someone you trust lies to you, cheats on you, abuses you, or hurts you by putting their own self-interest first.' It is quite simply hideous. I can't really comprehend how it ever comes about in any relationship that has lasted a very long time and I can't understand how you can continue to live with yourself when you decide to do the dirty deed. I also can't understand how you can live with yourself when you spend months telling lies, abusing and hurting someone you loved so wholeheartedly. I just don't get it. I have never betrayed anyone and nor do I ever intend to. It is against every fibre in my body. However, I now know that not everyone shares my moral code and my former wife obviously manages to live with herself quite comfortably. Maybe it's a case of the ends justifying the means. But it does make me question the authenticity of love, well, the authenticity of our love. I imagine the reason for my pain and heartache post-separation comes from my inability to accept the possibility of betrayal. I only thought it ever happened in Shakespearean tragedies, not in real life. Naive, silly me.

It's definitely part of life's learning curve. The funny thing is, I'm not tempted to change my own moral code, I just couldn't live with myself. I have to live with the aftermath of being betrayed for the rest of my life, I couldn't live with the guilt of betraying anyone I loved, that would be unbearable. I think it requires a coldness within that I just don't possess and one that I never wish to acquire. If you are like me, please stay true to yourself and those you love.

Narcissism

It must be terrible going through life with a lack of respect for other people. It's a kind of insensitivity that I find appalling and is based on total self-absorption. It is the ability to switch off when you are adversely affecting other people's lives in a cold and heartless fashion. I can't do it, but my ex certainly could.

I think that in its extreme cases, it's a form of mental sickness because nobody in their right mind should be capable of such cruelty. In my ex's case, it may well have been inherited as her mother has some severe personality disorders which are hard to fathom. She lacks empathy and the ability to read emotional signals…talk about a bull in a China shop. Yet these people often have the social graces to cover up their innate lack of compassion, appearing outwardly personable, but inwardly devious and totally untrustworthy. They can turn on you in a flash and devastate your life. However, you can spot the signs. If these people seem to be asking how you are and then immediately launch into a detailed explanation of how *they* are, beware. They aren't interested in you; they just want to talk about themselves. They also have an uncanny knack for finding what your weaknesses are and honing in on them with a steely determination that's quite shocking. The word 'evil' comes to mind.

I don't think it's necessary to be this sort of person in order to be successful at what you do in life. I don't think it's necessary to trample on the people around you in order to get ahead in life. In fact, quite the opposite. Empathy is the number one ingredient for any successful relationship. You have to be genuinely interested in people to work effectively with them. You have to care about what is best for them, not what is best for you. Besides, a dog-eat-dog attitude to life must be so damaging to the soul. It must rip you apart in the end and leave you devoid of feelings. The quest for money and material things at the expense of everyone around you is one expression of this, the quest for power is another. I have met so many of these people in my life and I just want to avoid them. In the end, they become very lonely and empty people.

If you happen to be in a relationship with a narcissist, you might find yourself being their next victim. Sadly, my ex became totally self-absorbed and everything in her life was about winning. It didn't matter what the collateral damage was, she just needed to win. Initially, it was about winning professionally, but ultimately, it was about winning in every aspect of her life and it didn't matter if she needed to lie, cheat, hurt or abandon anyone around her. It didn't matter how extreme her actions were and what the cost entailed. Now that must be a sickness.

Granted, we all have narcissistic tendencies because life is about self-preservation, we have to protect ourselves against external threats. But it does become a sickness when it's an obsession. It does become a sickness when you are unable to put yourself in the other person's shoes. You can't find common ground and have a meaningful relationship with anyone if you actually have no interest in them. My ex's mother is just like that. She doesn't even have any interest in her own daughter, above and beyond how her daughter reflects on her. Narcissism is deadly and unfortunately often runs in the family. One narcissist begets another and the evil dynasty continues.

It's a shame these people can go through life creating havoc wherever they go and leaving behind them a trail of broken hearts and damaged souls. I guess the trick is to try and spot the signs early and give them a wide berth. There really isn't any logical defence you can offer up because they are kamikaze pilots who will destroy themselves in order to destroy you. They will do anything to achieve what they want and the cost is unimportant. To be a narcissist, you have already destroyed a fundamental part of what makes you human: the ability to have empathy for your fellow man/woman.

Is it possible to love a narcissist? Of course, it is, because I for one fell into the trap. Often the signs remain dormant for a long time and we get lulled into a false sense of security by their outwardly charming demeanour. They can be quite lovely on the surface and even give the impression of caring about us. They may lavish us with gifts and pretend to want what's best for us, but in the end, everything is calculated with their own best interests in mind and the axe falls unceremoniously. I think they also have the ability to learn from one another. My ex became a narcissist by watching how her narcissistic mother works. Scary stuff for sure.

We just need to count our blessings when we are released from these despicable people. No good can ever become of the association if you want to retain any semblance of humanity yourself. I want to care about the people around me and I want to forge meaningful and reciprocal relationships with the people in my life. When they are happy, I'm happy. I don't need anything else.

Authenticity

Good morning, world! It's always a bonus having another day on this amazing planet. It's a privilege to be alive and one we shouldn't take for granted. Having made that bold statement, I've been feeling a bit guilty about the tone of my diary entries over the last few days because they've become a bit prescriptive and critical. I am the last person to be able to dictate what is the right or the wrong way to live life. I've screwed up my own in all manner of ways. The older I get, the less I seem to understand this adventure we are all on. But maybe I'm not alone in this respect; maybe we are all getting through life as best we can and will never understand what it's all about.

Of course, there seem to be people out there who manage to forge a very successful route through life without any major hiccups on the way. Everything just seems to fall into place for them, from schooling to work, to marriage, to family, to retirement. Neat and satisfactory chapters in a life well-lived. I'm glad for them and if it was all plain sailing, bully for them. However, I doubt that even the most outwardly idyllic cruise through life doesn't contain the odd storm leading to uncharted waters. That's one of the problems with social media, we are fed all the good bits. We read about these near-perfect lives, with their perfect pictures and their perfect fairy tale stories. Most of it is fake. We are being fed what these people want to feed us and the realities are quite different from the image presented. Unfortunately, these kinds of underhand tactics pervade society as a whole and we simply can't escape. We live in a fake world populated by fake people. Everyone is trying desperately to present an image of a perfect life, hell-bent on keeping up with the Joneses. Not only trying to keep up with the Joneses but wanting to be the Joneses. Flash houses, flash cars, 2.5 kids and the usual array of pets. All the outward trappings of success. Sadly, all of these fake things come at a price, not only a financial price but a dangerous personal one too.

In order to fit in, society demands these things from us. We are bombarded by fake representations of what we should aspire to achieve. It starts at school where peer pressure forces us to act and look in a certain way. We have to follow all the ridiculous trends in music and fashion in order to be 'cool.' We follow all of these things on social media and become brainwashed into thinking this is what life is all about. If we don't keep up with all the crap, we become outcasts and ostracized. It's insidious and very harmful and sometimes leads to tragic results. But, of course, it doesn't stop there, it carries on at university/college and then at work. Fit in or drop out, that's the modern-day mantra.

These sorts of societal pressures wreak havoc on relationships because they inflict a financial and cultural burden that isn't sustainable. Simple, heartfelt values are buried under a rockfall of pretence. People stop believing in themselves and start believing in the hyperbole. They stop believing in the authentic relationship they have with their partner and start yearning for a fairy-tale relationship with an ideal that doesn't exist. In the end, one fake life is traded for another fake life and the ridiculous cycle continues unabated.

I guess that's why my diary entries have become a bit prescriptive, critical and maybe a bit cynical. I'm trying to warn myself not to get wrapped up in all the puffery that is thrown my way. I am trying to stay true to myself and true to my new partner. My ex left my life for all the reasons I've written about today. She became consumed by this materialistic world and consumed by a perfect image of who she should be. My deep, profound and authentic love was not enough for her and she chose to spit on it and move on. Good luck to her in her new glass house. I can't wait 'til she starts throwing stones all over again.

I Am Not What Happened to Me, I Am What I Choose to Become

I can't remember who wrote these immortal words, but they kept me going for a long time after the split with my ex. Well, to be accurate, after she dumped me. Every day, the pain is still there in one form or another. Yesterday, I watched the new Bond movie and was reminded of her because we spent a night in the same Italian town where some of the opening scenes were shot. I guess the rest of my life is going to be like this, with constant reminders of my past cropping up to haunt me. Instead of being able to share them with the person I loved, they are now in the 'too hard to handle' category. The heartbreak still runs deep and I just hope it fades completely given time.

Fortunately, things are a lot better now. At one time, memory triggers like that would have thrown me into the depths of despair and it would have taken days or even weeks to recover. These days, I can air my feelings here and hopefully work through some of them. In previous entries, I've talked about regret, anger, longing, betrayal, abandonment and countless other highly charged emotional states. I've been through them all and felt their effects in a very tangible way—they have literally touched my soul. They have ravaged their way through me like some virus. I have also talked about mental illness and how pervasive it can be. I sometimes wonder if I have the strength to remain positive in the face of constant reminders from the past. I also wonder if I am the only one who feels this way after such a long period of time. Am I overly sensitive or too unbalanced to simply move on and leave all that garbage behind? Perhaps this pain from the past is a kind of mental sickness that won't go away? Why am I still writing about it and why am I still feeling the fallout after two and a half years?

Maybe one day, I will be able to answer these questions, but luckily, these moments of weakness pass if I continue to block the memories; I must keep up the good work. I must keep repeating to myself the title of this entry: 'I am not what happened to me, I am what I choose to become.' These are very powerful words and words I will probably take to my grave. These sorts of events in our lives inevitably change us. They make us different people. Maybe they even make us stronger in the long run. But the process is still a long and challenging one, at least for someone like me. However, I am so much stronger than I used to be and that's another thing I need to keep reminding myself about. There might be the odd chinks in my armour but on the whole, I can cope with so much more. I bounce back quicker and spend less time in a state of helplessness. It's called greater resilience, I suppose.

I'm sorry to inflict all these maybes on you today, but like most of these entries, I'm trying to feel my way forwards. Heartbreak Hotel is a very dark place to inhabit. In the initial stages, there isn't any light at all and we end up fumbling our way around in the pitch black unable to make sense of anything. Nothing feels right and nothing is recognisable to the touch. Our first year of occupancy is marked by a kind of world blindness; we just can't make sense of anything anymore. One day morphs into another and we still don't know where we are and what we are supposed to do to escape. Occasionally, we see a glimmer of light and head towards it, only to find it's gone when we get there. It's like trying to find the end of a rainbow. That elusive pot of gold is so tantalising but so nefarious too. Wickedly tempting, but ultimately unattainable. The second year of fumbling around in Heartbreak Hotel can once again bring moments of hope. At least, we are beginning to recognise what we are feeling. We might not be able to see the light, but what we feel makes more sense. Eventually, those glimmers of light become less mirages and more gateways to freedom. After years of emotional darkness, we begin to see the light and it's time to check out of Heartbreak Hotel for good.

It's a nice story, but I'm not so sure about the ending just yet. *Maybe* it's just too soon for me? What I do know is that all that time in the dark exploring my feelings has definitely made me a more resourceful person. I may not have seen the light completely, but at least I know the difference between what I see now compared with those mirages of the past. I might still need to revisit Heartbreak Hotel occasionally, but I sure as hell don't want to live there anymore.

Luck

It's another one of those sleepless nights, so I'm up writing my diary pretty early in the day. I'll probably be a bit the worse for wear when the sun rises but such is life. Sometimes, thoughts just have a habit of whirring around and no matter how you try, you can't put them to rest and get back to sleep. These days, I just go with the flow and see what happens.

I have absolutely no idea what life is all about. Over the years, I've tried to make sense of it and I've tried my best to keep those around me happy. I've been blessed in so many ways in terms of the people I've met and the experiences I've had. I've probably had a very lucky life and for that, I'm really grateful. However, as I negotiate the rest of it, I'm struck by the need to find a purpose. For years, my purpose was to support and care for my ex, it was the thing that kept me going. When she decided enough was enough and moved on, my world collapsed around me and it's been very difficult to glue it back together. Fortunately, I've been lucky once again and I've found a wonderful woman to share the rest of my life with. The difficulty is letting go of one part of your life and forging ahead with another. We tend to spend a good deal of time with one leg in the past and one leg in the future and when the two worlds gradually separate, we end up doing the splits. It can be painful.

I think I've probably got a little more weight on the future leg now and I'm desperately trying to yank the past leg over the ever-widening void. If I successfully complete this manoeuvre, I'll be able to stand on my own two feet. I guess that's a good purpose in life. My partner and I were talking about this over a few bottles of wine last night. My partner is a very wise woman and a very understanding one too. I was trying to explain to her that I'm finding it difficult to let go of the ex I married, not the ex that dumped me twenty years later. The first version was kind, warm and compassionate; the second was cruel, cold and heartless. The leg that's still gripping onto the past with one toe, is gripping onto the memory of my ex as she was during the good times that we shared. What my partner so graciously and intelligently pointed out, was that my ex's final act of love—although it didn't seem that way at the time—was letting me go so that I could find an amazing woman to share the last part of my life with. I couldn't agree more. I'm coming to realise that I probably couldn't have survived living with the woman my ex had become. I'm also coming to realise I've been incredibly lucky; my ex's cruelty has actually allowed me to meet the kind, warm and compassionate woman she used to be. I didn't think I'd ever be saying anything like that. But, of course, my new partner is so much more than kind, warm and compassionate, she is also incredibly wise. Yes, I'm a very lucky man.

The moral of today's story is that fate has a funny way of helping things turn out for the best, we just need to be patient and let it do its thing. We also need to be careful not to second-guess it. We can only do the splits for a certain amount of time before we do ourselves some permanent damage. With a bit of luck, we can all find that special person to grab our hand and pull us safely into the future.

Pollock

Sometimes, it's a scary business staring at a blank page. I imagine abstract painters face the same challenges. Do you think of a theme before mixing the paint or just launch in and see what happens? I certainly favour the latter approach. The themes usually take care of themselves once the first splash of paint lands and the first paragraph is behind you.

In my former life, I remember visiting the studio of Jackson Pollock in East Hampton, on Long Island, New York. The place is now known as Pollock-Krasner House as Jackson and his artist wife Lee Krasner bought the place in 1945 with financial help from Peggy Guggenheim. Guggenheim gave Pollock the $2000 down payment on the house in exchange for all the work he created in his first two years there. With hindsight, it was another great Guggenheim investment as Pollock became one of America's greatest painters and the leading light in the abstract expressionist movement. Peggy was good at spotting a genius, but also all too aware of their weaknesses. After Pollock drank too much and peed into a fireplace at one of her influential parties, she thought it was probably a good idea to send him to a place where he could focus on his work and his heavy drinking would not be too much of a problem. Sadly, his fondness for the turps eventually caught up with him and he died in a drink-related car crash at the age of 44.

I've been a big fan of Jackson Pollock ever since that Hamptons visit. His style of painting was large-scale. He'd climb up a ladder and drip the paint onto a large canvas below, earning him the amusing nickname of 'Jack the Dripper.' I like the randomness of this approach and absolutely love the end results. If I had a spare few million, I'd have one of his works hanging in my living room. It just goes to show that Oscar Wilde was right when he wrote: 'Without order, nothing can exist, without chaos, nothing can evolve.' We are all evolving in one way or another and often chaos certainly helps us along our way.

I think I've had enough of order in my life. We can become a slave to it. The greatest achievements in the world have been the result of bucking trends, not following them. Jackson Pollock had the tenacity to think outside the box and produce work that was stunningly original. We should all aspire to that sort of creativity in whatever field we work in. I think we should also take the same approach to our personal relationships. In a previous entry, I talked about the pressures of keeping up with the Joneses and how damaging this can become. Following a blueprint for life leads to mediocrity and hum-drum relationships that lack the spark of creativity. A relationship should be a living and ever-evolving entity, not a stagnant pond. We need to take a chance with it and let chaos help us grow and evolve together.

Blips

I need to be honest in these diary entries otherwise there isn't a great deal of point in writing them. Well, after a pretty good run of 56 days, I have been feeling a bit down. I've tried to convince myself it wasn't happening, but the signals have been there. I've caught myself dwelling on negative thoughts and bit by bit, they've dragged me down. I've been letting the subtle little triggers take hold without instantly blocking them and it's had a cumulative effect on my mood. I start to question everything in my life.

I'm really hoping that I can take control again before things get out of hand. These negative thoughts are so insidious. They pop into your mind randomly and you only need to dwell on them for a couple of seconds for the damage to be done. One thought on its own isn't the problem, but it's the start of the rot. The negative part of our mind sees an opportunity and grabs it. One moment of weakness leads to another and before we know it, we've been dragged back to dark places we thought we'd well and truly left behind. It also affects my health as my blood pressure goes up and I know this is very bad for me. Then I start worrying about that and it makes things worse.

Today is going to be a day of reaffirming my blocking techniques. Every single time a negative thought comes into my mind, I'm going to block it and think about something completely different. I can't really understand how I managed to let my guard down, but I did and I need to do something about it. I know that by writing these things down, I'm helping to strengthen my resolve which is a very good thing and even now, I'm feeling a bit better. I've got to be more careful. I mustn't abandon all the good work I've done over the last couple of months, it's crazy.

In a way, I should be grateful for this blip in my mental state because it has made me aware that I can't afford to become complacent. We often live our lives on a knife edge and it doesn't take much to revert back to old bad habits. Maybe they are full of ever-so-familiar thoughts that have a sort of comfort attached to them. They seem to be inviting us back like old friends filling us with the euphoria of past times. Tempting us to relive a pleasant memory and lulling us into a false sense of security. We go like lambs to the slaughter and end up right back in that horribly dark place full of regret, sadness and longing. If we go all the way, our life becomes pointless and we can't see any way forward.

Why do we indulge in this self-annihilation, it's ridiculous. I think there are many factors involved. General physical health plays its part. If we are feeling a bit under the weather, it is very easy to lapse into thoughts about the past and give in to those negative triggers that crop up everywhere. When the weather is bad, I tend to feel a bit down and can't get out for my regular walks. Maybe someone close to us is feeling down? Maybe some of our plans have been delayed? They are all things that can eat away at our undertaking to blot out negative thoughts and leave us open to their cumulative effects.

I'm not going to do it. I am not going to go down that appalling road of self-destruction and end up thinking there is nothing left for me in life. Every single time a negative thought comes into my mind, or I have a memory flashback, I'm going to block it and think of something positive and uplifting. I am not going to get back onto that negative treadmill, life is just too darn short.

Balance

Greetings for the second time today. After my entry this morning, I tried to put all my blocking techniques into play and also went for a long walk. I feel better and my blood pressure has gone down a bit. I still have some way to go with that, but I'm hoping after a relaxing afternoon and a lot of positive thought energy, it will be back to normal by the end of the day. Mental stress and negativity have a huge effect on our bodily functions and can be the cause of all manner of ailments. I am determined to explore every avenue to keep this delicate body of mine running smoothly. It's all a matter of balance.

It doesn't take much for us to lose equilibrium. The odd throw-away comment from someone can just wreak havoc with our guidance systems. I was reading a post by an artist friend of mine and she was mentioning how upset she got when she overheard some people making unkind comments about her work at a recent exhibition. They didn't know she was behind them, so they proceeded to launch into a tirade about how awful the painting was and how could it possibly be priced so high. My friend is an experienced abstract artist and I know for sure her work could never be described as awful. Some people just can't cope with anything they don't understand and are usually too stupid to try. If they could only open their eyes and their minds the world would be a much better place. For some people, life is black-and-white and that's all there is to it.

I think artists are particularly vulnerable to the black-and-white brigade. When something is subjective, beauty will always be in the eye of the beholder. There will never be a right or a wrong way of doing anything. In fact, as I mentioned the other day, Oscar Wilde hit the nail on the head when he said 'nothing can evolve without chaos.' It takes courage to experiment and not follow the rules. It takes courage to be your authentic self and rely on your instincts for guidance. Artists need to develop thick skins in order to survive. But a thick skin doesn't necessarily go with the territory. Artists are generally sensitive souls who are riddled with self-doubt and one unkind word can really set the cat amongst the pigeons.

Of course, this kind of self-doubt isn't only the domain of the artist, we all suffer from it in one form or another. We doubt our choices in life and we doubt our ability to follow through with them. This kind of indecision can lead to flitting from one job to another and sometimes flitting from one relationship to another in the vain hope of finding perfection. Perfection is in the eye of the beholder; it has nothing to do with being right or wrong. My artist friend needs to ignore the naysayers who can't appreciate her talent and find people who do. She needs to find people who appreciate her authentic talent, one which comes from the heart. Likewise, we all need to trust our instincts and surround ourselves with people who appreciate our uniqueness, just as we appreciate their uniqueness.

My struggles to eliminate negativity are probably a reflection of my own self-doubt and inability to come to terms with the direction my life has taken, either through my own decisions or the decisions of those around me. I keep looking back and wondering what would have happened if I had made different decisions; if I had made different choices. The trouble with that kind of activity is that it is self-perpetuating, the more you think about it, the more doubt creeps in. It's equivalent to my painter friend questioning every brushstroke she makes until she's actually too afraid to continue. Akin to the writer never being able to find the next word for fearing not making perfect sense. In the end, the only real perfection is not to do anything. Don't paint, don't write and ultimately don't breathe.

Black-and-white people destroy creativity because they are hell-bent on inflicting perfection on those around them. They spend the whole of their lives looking for reasons to complain and criticise. They are life's observers and commentators who have nothing original to contribute because they have nothing original to say. They can regurgitate rules and regulations till the cows come home, but they can't take anything on board and make it their own. For me—and I know this will sound a trifle pathetic—these people are usually the ones who honk their car horns when anyone makes the slightest inappropriate manoeuvre. They must drive along with their hands on the horn button, poised for action. Whenever I've been exasperated and tempted to honk, I can never find the button, so unaccustomed am I to such petty-minded outbursts. We all make mistakes in life and driving isn't exempt. Those honkers should remember the last time they cut someone up themselves.

I think in life, we need to cut ourselves some slack and do the same for those around us. If we can forgive ourselves, we'll be better able to forgive others. Live and let live, go with the flow and make the best decisions we can, based on the information we have. No second-guessing, no recriminations. Life is unpredictable, outcomes are unpredictable and if we are unpredictable, that's fine too. I need to accept that I'll probably never be 100% happy or totally depression-free, but that doesn't matter, what matters is that I don't beat myself up about it but try to restore some balance as best I can, whenever I can.

Taking Stock

In recent entries, I've drifted away from the main purpose of this diary which is to try to recover from the end of a long-term relationship over two and a half years ago. I really can't believe I am still working my way through all of this after so much time. But I am, and despite all my best efforts, I just don't seem to be able to let it go. This morning, I caught myself waking up to those sinking feelings of loss and regret in the very pit of my stomach, feelings that no amount of time seems to heal. Over the last few months, I've written extensively about these feelings and have often managed to tame them and find logical ways to circumvent them, but they keep coming back.

Of course, the root of the problem lies in the fact that I didn't end the relationship, my ex did. The feelings of betrayal are profound because in the course of 24 years together, I never cheated on her, I always respected her and I always looked out for her. The way she ended our relationship was nothing short of cruel and heartbreaking. She made no attempt to save our marriage by going to counselling and simply had an affair, committed adultery and moved on. She also treated me with utter contempt in the process and ripped me to shreds emotionally. She lied to me for months and continued the lies after we separated. Her lies have left me without any mutual friends and in their eyes, the guilty party. It is disgusting and I will never forgive her. I have no idea how she lives with herself or how she justifies any of her actions in her own mind.

But this sort of an outburst doesn't really help me. Somehow, I need to find a way to live with the situation and move on. I just can't understand how anyone could be so cold and callous after such a long period of time. Yes, I acknowledge I am no angel and I have faults like everyone, but my heart was always in the right place and it was firmly wrapped up in her. I can't let go because I can't really believe what happened. I can't understand such betrayal because I'm not capable of it myself. However, I need to accept that other people are not me. More importantly, I need to understand that my ex stopped loving me and that is something beyond my control. And even more importantly, I need to stop blaming myself for what happened.

Towards the end of our marriage, everything was my fault, or at least, that's the way it seemed. Maybe some of it was, but *everything*? Somehow, I doubt it. I did everything I could to make her happy, but that obviously wasn't enough. Of course, I should have done more and that contributes to the self-blame, but did I really deserve to be dumped so heartlessly? Well, obviously in her mind, yes. Life is always about choices and I have the choice of living my life to the full with my new partner or wallowing in my own regrets and blaming myself for everything. I must choose the former as the latter is a prison sentence nobody wants.

The funny thing is that my new partner doesn't blame me for anything, in fact, quite the opposite. She thanks me for being kind, caring and considerate and always supportive of her. All the things I was for my ex. Maybe I am not quite the monster my ex made me out to be towards the end. To be honest, it was quite difficult loving my ex when she became such an incredible bully—although I never faltered regardless. When she became so full of her own self-importance, she couldn't value the person closest to her. Career, money and social standing became all she was interested in. In hindsight, she chewed up and spat out a number of her colleagues and I always thought it was their fault. She even turned on her own mother—but as I've pointed out previously, her mother was one of her biggest problems, so I understand that. Fortunately, my wonderful new partner values all the important things in life, not the glitz and glam of a fake world. She is far more accomplished and talented than my ex and yet she retains a wonderful modesty and respect for other people. Whilst at the top of her profession, she isn't interested in money or social standing, she just wants to help people. I am very, very lucky that she wants to share her life with me.

I think the end of the last paragraph says it all. I am an incredibly lucky man because I have now met someone who shares all my own values. My ex lost touch with who I am and what I hold dear. She lost touch with my core values and what used to be her core values. I must stop blaming myself for whom my ex *became* and start celebrating who my new partner *is*. I think I've been saying this over and over again in the last couple of months, I simply must take it on board. Unfortunately, it's in my nature to try to accept responsibility for everything and in a way that was something I learned to do with my ex. She is still controlling me just as long as I keep blaming myself for what happened. I need to remind myself I didn't change, she did. I need to remind myself I am so incredibly lucky to now have someone in my life who values what I value and who is as kind and considerate as I try to be.

Swap Shoes

I think yesterday's diary entry was a good one because it highlighted a very important aspect of our lives: being grateful for what we have in the here and now. So often we become fixated on finding something better and forget to value what we already have. It's the old feeling that the grass is always greener in the next field. I've seen cows do it. They are already in a lush paddock and yet are still struggling to get their heads through the fence to the grass next door. Maybe it's a component of being alive, maybe it's what keeps us alive. At any rate, it often backfires.

The trouble with not being happy with our current situation in life is that it makes us either dream about a non-existent future or wallow in an idealised past. Both places are not real. What is real, is the here and now and if we just made the effort to make the most of what we have, we might be very surprised at what we find. I'm not talking about 'making do' with something that's not working, I'm talking about looking at things in a new light. Sometimes, all it takes is a change of perspective to understand a situation better. In terms of relationships, it's the ability to put yourself in the other person's shoes. So often we get hell-bent on feeling short-changed, and we forget to consider that there are always two sides to the story. If both people can step back for a few moments and look at things holistically, the relationship will be given the opportunity to flourish again. But it must be a conscious and open effort on both sides.

In my failed relationship, my ex did all her processing internally. In her mind, she obviously gave me heaps of chances to change and when I didn't, she decided to move on. I didn't know what was going on. I imagined that her unhappiness was due to all manner of external influences and nothing to do with our—what I believed to be—rock-solid marriage. In that respect, I need to take responsibility for not picking up the signs. But I can't really blame myself for not being able to read her mind. Unfortunately, in a long-term relationship, we think our partner should know what we are thinking and feeling instinctively. We think that they can predict our every thought and when they don't act on this prediction, they are deliberately not paying us the attention we deserve. We become hurt and indignant and this leads us to believe that the grass might be greener elsewhere. Maybe it is, maybe it isn't, but it's a huge step to take and the emotional fallout can be severe.

With hindsight, my advice to anyone who is facing this sort of scenario is to try and find a way to communicate again. Stop second-guessing each other and start talking openly about how you think things could move forward. Swap shoes and see how it feels. It might be that one or both of your thought processes have gone too far down the 'grass is always greener' track for reconciliation, but believe me, in the future, you'll both regret not giving it a try.

Sink or Swim

I don't really know how to start today's entry because I feel like a failure. After a couple of months of keeping the dreaded depression at bay, I've found myself slipping back into my old bad habits of revisiting the past. It started with a few triggers that I couldn't resist following through on and ended up with me staying awake in the middle of the night and wondering what on earth is the point of my life. It is ridiculous and so destructive. I am going to have to start back at square one with my blocking techniques and hope I can pull myself through all over again.

However, one of the things I've learnt from this whole experience is that nothing is plain sailing, there are always going to be setbacks in life and it's how we deal with them that can make us sink or swim. I must be proud of what I have achieved in two months and make every effort to build on those victories. But these feelings of worthlessness are crippling. It's as if all the fight has gone out of me; I just haven't got the energy to pick myself up yet again. Whatever I think about seems pointless. All my dreams and plans are now empty and hollow.

I must pull myself out of this hole before it swallows me up completely. I've been a lot deeper in the past, so I know I can do it, one step at a time. Firstly, I must remind myself that I have a lot to be thankful for. I am healthy and I have a wonderfully supportive partner. I may miss my former life terribly, but I do have a new life ahead of me if only I choose to put the past behind me. Secondly, I must be more accepting of the vagaries of life. I need to realise that for me, the recovery process is going to be a very long one. There may be a lot of two steps forward and one back, but at least I'll always be at least one step ahead.

When I'm at a low ebb, it is so easy to give up. I have even thought about giving up on this diary. It's so easy to admit defeat and throw everything away. But this doesn't achieve anything other than more heartache. Defeat begets defeat and contributes to an even bigger fall. At times like this, I need to be honest with myself and understand that I am not the only person in the world who is feeling this way. I need to remind myself that after every time in my life I've felt this way, there have been brighter times ahead. After every down, there is an up. I probably need to read all my diary entries again and actually see how much I've grown in the last couple of months.

Every new day gives us the opportunity to be a new person. I can become the person I want to be if I can only latch onto what is really important to me now. I can become the person I want to be if I can only focus on the people I love and who love me. I am wasting the rest of my life by focusing on those who have gone. I'm actually feeling a bit better already. I'll go and give my wonderful partner a hug.

Look for a Lifeline

I had a good sleep last night and dreamt about all manner of things. There were a few anxiety dreams but nothing serious enough to wake me up. In fact, although I was fretting about getting a task done which I didn't know anything about, I took it in my stride and the situation seemed to resolve itself. I'm hoping this sort of resolution will be reflected in my conscious life.

Sometimes, it's a matter of biding our time and waiting for the storms to pass. It takes patience and a certain amount of courage to sit these things out. It also helps if we have a post-storm action plan formalised in our minds. Unfortunately, storms tend to push us off course and in the midst of all the mayhem, it's difficult to think clearly. But having a rough idea of where we'll be heading always helps as it adds a much-needed focus. I'm a great believer in having this kind of game plan. I try to cover the destiny options in my mind: If the storm brings me here, this is what I'll do. If the storm brings me there, that's what I'll do. Even if the storm brings me somewhere I can't predict, I'll have a strategy for coping with that situation as well.

Of course, this sort of thing is only very vague because we can never really predict how our life is going to work out and whom we might meet on the way. Being thrown a lifeline by a complete stranger is one of life's magical moments. It restores our faith in humanity and gives us the feeling that even when we're at our lowest ebb, we are still worth saving. I know I'm going a bit overboard (there I go again) with these nautical metaphors, but I think it helps to make the point. Fortunately, we are never alone as long as we make ourselves open to assistance. We need to grab the lifeline in order to survive. Moreover, we need to consciously look for it.

When my relationship failed, I was a complete and utter mess. I was definitely a rudderless ship with no sense of direction or any sense of what I should do. But deep down, I knew I needed to look out for those lifelines and surround myself with people who could get me back on track. My closest family helped enormously and even a few valued friends were good enough to listen. But what helped me most of all was a burning desire to meet someone who could restore my faith in womankind. My ex had set me adrift in such a traumatic and vile way, I needed reassurance that I was still worthy of another person's love despite what she may have thought. This quest became my whole purpose in life and led to the wonderful woman I share my life with now. It didn't even require a plethora of interim relationships. I went on two dates (just dinner) between my ex and my partner. I always wanted to be a one-woman man, but my ex made sure that wouldn't be the case, so a two-woman man it is.

I think it's all about giving ourselves an escape route and never allowing a feeling of hopelessness to set in. I do that with negative thoughts now. It's like a superior counter punch. It's about creating a better situation for yourself than the one you find yourself in. Every cloud has a silver lining if we only look for it. Every storm has a lifeline there to grab. Every failed relationship has a better one waiting in the wings; we just have to look hard enough.

Dodo

I was thinking recently wouldn't it be nice if we could go somewhere to get certain parts of our memory erased? We could have selective brainwashing in its purest sense. I could have everything concerning my ex expunged from my brain and then live happily ever after—wouldn't it be lovely! I guess the nearest I'm going to get to this sort of liberation is by trying to block the memories and therefore not reinforcing the neural pathways that keep them alive. If I can do this enough, with a bit of luck they will wither away and die. The only trouble with this radical approach is that you end up wiping out a whole chunk of your life. It's pretty drastic surgery on my relatively brief appearance on this planet. There must be another way…

If only I could learn to live with the memories but not let them upset me. If I could just keep emotionally detached and enjoy them for what they are, rather than become a blubbering wreck every time I revisit them. Chance would be a fine thing. Am I living in cloud-cuckoo-land? Or is it just a matter of time? So many questions, so few answers.

Anyone reading this diary will realise I spend a lot of time going around in circles. I have been down so many different avenues off this recovery highway that I can hardly tell which ones I've visited and which ones I'm yet to explore. One moment, I feel I'm making progress, the next I'm doubting I've got anywhere. It can be very confusing and frustrating. There just doesn't seem to be an easy route out of such a major emotional trauma. I also feel like a fraud trying to pass on my words of wisdom when I don't really have any. All I have is endless doubt and huge amounts of unanswered questions.

Today is another one of those days where nothing really makes sense. I woke up early and started thinking about my previous life, but at least I know what triggered it. A good friend had accidentally sent a package to my old address and as my PO redirection service ended ages ago, I needed to contact the new owner to get them to send it on. I ended up having a phone conversation with them and that led to a predictable rehashing of the past. Not the best of scenarios, but not something I could really avoid. One thought led to another and off I went whizzing down memory lane, thought after thought flashing by and making me more depressed at every glance. Crazy me.

I've just got to admit it, today's entry is a washout. It has no theme; it has no cohesion and it doesn't make any sense at all. It may as well be extinct. Hopefully, I'll get back on track tomorrow…à *bientôt*.

States of Mind

We had some friends around last night for a BBQ and I think I overindulged in the vino. I had a horrible headache for most of the night and although I've recovered now, I still feel a bit under the weather. The dreaded grog has hit again and I wonder if I'll ever learn. It's so nice at the time and when you have relaxed and engaging company, it's easy to go a bit overboard. Not to worry, onwards and upwards and it will be good to have a quiet night this evening.

In the course of my sleepless and headache-infused night, I thought about writing quite a bit. I thought about how therapeutic the whole process has become and how much I look forward to my time with words. I guess the words themselves are pretty meaningless, but the thoughts that they convey have a liberating effect. Ideas are always buzzing around in my head and unless I have an escape valve for them, they can become overpowering. I'm not sure if I have an overly active mind or if I'm just like everyone else. Perhaps, most people are plagued by the same affliction or is it really an affliction anyway? Throughout my life, I've had this strange idea that we all create our own worlds. After all, there is a lot of truth in the phrase, *I think, therefore I am*. This idea put Descartes on the philosophical map and quite rightly so. So, all these buzzing thoughts are what makes me, well, me. If my head was a vacuum, would there be any point in my existence? Are we just vegetables if we don't think? Cogito, ergo sum, has its problems of course because there are many examples of people not being able to think through accidents, degenerative diseases or even when in a coma. These people do exist, even if they have lost the capacity to think.

Of course, I'm not a philosopher, so I can't really comment on such complicated concepts, but they certainly give me food for thought nonetheless. What I find fascinating is that if we can gain control over our minds, we can gain control of our state. Moreover, if we can harness our thought processes, we can relieve ourselves of unhealthy states. The challenge for me then is to gather all of those random buzzing thoughts into some semblance of order and try to make sense of them. It's akin to a musician gathering up all manner of different pitches and putting them together into some sort of order. A good tune has a recognisable beginning, middle and end. Randomness is less satisfying.

I imagine what I'm trying to say is that I have the choice to think about whatever I want to think about. If I choose to dwell on negative thoughts that upset me, I have made that choice. Out of all the thoughts whirring around in my head at one given time, I've decided to select those and make some sense of them. Unfortunately, I don't have the ability to think about negative and positive thoughts simultaneously, so the negative thoughts are going to put me into a negative state. If I choose to pick out the positive thoughts whirring around in my brain, I'd end up in a positive state. It sounds simple, but putting it into practice is the hard bit.

Writing down my thoughts takes the randomness out of the equation. I can select thoughts deliberately to form a cogent argument. I can create a logical tune that's memorable. I also have the choice to dwell on uplifting topics, rather than depressing ones. I can choose to ameliorate my mood or intensify its darker side. Writing my thoughts down gives me greater control over my overall state. We all have the ability to change our state instantly, so if we are feeling down or unhappy, we should choose to pick out happy and uplifting thoughts from those buzzing synapses. We should smile and think about all the good things in our lives. Better still, write them all down. We'll feel much better in no time at all.

Misplaced Loyalty

Today, I want to focus on why we feel so empty when a long-term relationship fails and why we just can't seem to let go and move on. Part of the problem involves the expectation that the person we shared such a long period of time with, will always be there. It's as if any new experience we have in life is invalid because we are not sharing it with them. It's a ludicrous scenario and one that keeps us in a state of emotional stagnation. It also smacks of continued emotional control and we must break free of this if we stand any chance of making a new life for ourselves.

I've talked in the past about my ex being a control freak and how this grip tightened year in, year out. In the end, when she asked my opinion about something I always knew, she'd do the exact opposite or find reasons why she didn't agree with my choice. My solution was to go along with anything she said because it saved a whole lot of time. I became a 'yes man' and I stopped thinking for myself. When this happens, you become totally reliant on your partner and although you may not always agree with their decisions, you acquiesce anyway. I became programmed into this sort of reaction. I also thought I was doing the best thing for our relationship.

With hindsight, I was far too weak. I was so concerned about not rocking the boat, the whole thing sank in the process. But those years of supplication have left their mark and I'm finding it difficult to regain my independence. When the person you relied upon for everything suddenly exits from your life, it leaves a gaping hole. Over twenty years of associated memories keep popping back and somehow your mind wants your new experiences to go into the same folder. You start to wonder how any new experience can really be good unless it's shared with your ex. For such a long period of time, your life was mapped out to contain this person. Your future was inexorably linked to this person. All your hopes and dreams contained this person. You and this person were one.

I sometimes feel like Hachi the dog (Hachi: A Dog's Tale. 2009), who pined away for his master, constantly waiting at the railway station, year in, year out. It's so sad. The difference is, Hachi's master was lovely and sadly dies of a stroke, mine betrayed me and went off with someone else. My loyalty is totally misplaced and I must wake up to this or I'll spend the rest of my life waiting at the station too. Loyalty is a two-way thing and it requires devotion on both sides to work.

I've been given an amazing opportunity to share my life with a wonderful new partner who is loving and loyal. Rather than pining for someone who betrayed me, I must celebrate my good fortune and make new memories with her.

Renewed Resolve

It's been a difficult week with my diary. I have lost direction and started to regress into old, bad habits. My blocking techniques which started off so well slipped from my grasp and I have started to go over a lot of old ground. However, I'm back with a vengeance after giving myself a good talking to and I'm going to start again in the hope that my resolve will last a little bit longer this time around.

No matter how much I loved my ex, I must remind myself that she left me and triggered the most heartbreaking time in my life. I must also remind myself that the loyalty I gave her for over twenty years is null and void now. I have absolutely no reason to retain any feelings for her, particularly after the abominable way she treated me towards the end of our marriage. My loyalty must now be towards my wonderful new partner who has stood by me for the last two years, constantly supporting, comforting and loving me. She is the most important person in this equation, not some fanciful memory of someone who has long since gone and forged their own new life with probably not a thought for my feelings or wellbeing. That person has gone and good riddance.

Every time I am tempted to think back, I now think about my new partner and how lucky I am to be sharing my life with her. Every backward thought is an insult to her and what she has done for me. Let's face it, everything in life can be a trigger if I let it be a trigger. I must realise that if I spend my life in the past getting miserable, it's a choice that I have made, not one that my awful ex has made for me. She is gone and doesn't have any influence over me whatsoever unless I let her ghost rule my life. Everybody experiences loss at some point in their lives and it is how we deal with that loss that makes all the difference. I think one of the reasons I have found this whole experience so devastating is that it came to me relatively late in life. I married late after very little experience in dating. I was always looking for that one and only perfect match; one I would be with for the rest of my life. I had never had my heart broken because I didn't want to get involved with anyone I wasn't totally committed to, or who wasn't totally committed to me. It was idealistic and stupid, but that's me. I thought I had found her, but after 24 years together, it wasn't to be.

I've been lucky because this is my only broken heart, many people experience these feelings multiple times throughout their lives. It must be awful. But maybe when it happens more than once, you can be more prepared for it and develop some techniques to make the pain less biting. Not that I'm expecting to have a broken heart ever again. I'm not sure I could cope. I certainly intend to remain loyal to my new partner come what may, because that is who I am. I have never betrayed anyone and I never will. Loyalty is the core of my moral code. Without trust and commitment what sort of a relationship would it be? You need to be able to trust your partner implicitly and with that trust comes a security that is blissful. My ex is a betrayer. She can bury her actions as much as she likes and lie to herself and everyone around her, but hopefully, the immense pain she has caused will come back to haunt her. She didn't deserve my love and loyalty and I hope she eventually realises how cruel she became.

But as I said before, all of this is meaningless now and whilst divine retribution sounds quite appealing, it isn't something I think about a lot. My energies are best channelled into making a life with my new partner who has shown me love in abundance. Our life together is stress-free because it is not a competition but a true partnership. We respect each other for what we can bring to the relationship. We have different strengths which we celebrate rather than denigrate. We negotiate, not compete. Isn't that the way it should be? We also share the same core beliefs of loyalty, trust and compassion. My ex turned her back on these and that hardly bodes well for her future.

Faustian Bargain

In the last few months, I've been watching back-to-back episodes of the American legal drama, Suits. After eight seasons, the main characters are pretty well-formed and it's obvious they all have their own hang-ups in one form or another. It's actually very difficult to get through life unscathed and neurosis free. Coming to terms with these impediments can be a life-long undertaking and actually resolving them is exceedingly difficult.

But the first part of resolution always involves acknowledging they exist. So often we take the Ostrich approach and bury our heads in the sand. We don't want to own up to our weaknesses and will do anything to present to the world our infallibility. Unfortunately, such pride always comes before a fall and we have to face the reality of our situation regardless. Life is a journey and we should try to learn from our mistakes, but sadly, we often keep on making them. I am still looking back when I should be looking forward. I am still raking over things from the past that has no relevance to my life today. Maybe it's a matter of breaking the cycle gradually and not expecting a world-shattering transformation overnight.

The characters in Suits keep facing the same demons over and over again. Harvey can't forgive his mother for betraying his father, Mike can't cope with the loss of his parents at an early age and Louis has so many chips on his shoulder, it's hard to know where to start. However, one of the most interesting characters is Donna, Harvey's legal secretary and confidant. She is proud and assured and quite obviously in love with her boss and him with her. Their constant denial of this chemistry borders on tragedy, but it also highlights their basic inability to commit. Harvey doesn't trust women, but most importantly, those closest to him. Donna doesn't trust men because her father let the whole family down when she was a child by losing his job. These doubts and insecurities pervade their relationship and stop them moving forward and enjoying their lives together. If only we could be honest with ourselves and open the doors to being honest with our loved ones.

I think one of the reasons I'm finding it so hard to accept my ex's betrayal is that my mother was so loyal and committed to my father. She gave me the blueprint for a stable marriage. She was devoted to him and he to her. Despite many traumatic times in their lives, they stayed together and provided a loving home for their children. I was brought up to believe that's what you did and that's what true love is all about. I realise a lot of what I remember is seen through rose-coloured spectacles, but nonetheless, I can honestly say I never felt insecure. Even the hardships were character-building rather than demoralising. We didn't have much materialistically, but what we had emotionally was far more important. Even though I always had a burning desire to achieve things, I never felt pressured by my parents to succeed. Of course, they were proud if I did manage to stand out, but that was never their main concern. They wanted me to be happy in whatever I did.

My role model was therefore a woman who loved her husband and her children, but most importantly, her husband, first and foremost. I remember her telling me that on one occasion, and I was entirely comfortable with it. In fact, to me, it represented a confirmation of the family unit. My brothers may have had a different relationship with her, but that was mine. I guess as I moved on through life, I was looking for a woman with similar characteristics. It's the classic case of a man marrying a woman like his mother and a woman marrying a man like her father.

My ex came from a completely different background. Her parents had an open marriage which was absolutely abhorrent to me. Whilst they looked after their only daughter well in terms of materialistic things, emotionally she was scarred from an early age. You can't possibly feel secure when your parents are openly seeing other people, it's a recipe for disaster. However, her father was a kind and considerate man and I think she saw a lot of him in me. She, therefore, married a man like her father. I think I provided the kind of totally loyal and stable environment my ex craved for. She could be assured I would be there for her through thick and thin. Unfortunately, after 24 years, she craved more. Materialistic things became more important than emotional stability. Perhaps, she wondered why she couldn't have both. But loyalty isn't like that, it's there or it's not. Love isn't like that, it's there or it's not. Hardship should bring people

155

who love each other together, not drive them apart. Ultimately, my ex made a Faustian bargain and I can only hope for her sake, it has been worth it.

So many people go through life sacrificing their souls for materialistic things. To me, it's an impossible trade. Eventually, you'll be eaten alive by your weakness and sully everyone around you. You may think you are living the life of Riley, but by selling your soul to the devil, you'll end up being nothing more than an empty shell. Without integrity, we are nothing.

I may be struggling to come to terms with being betrayed, but I'm as sure as hell I'd be struggling more if I had done the betraying. I'm glad my parents instilled in me a sense of what is right and what is wrong. I need to remind myself constantly that I may be beating myself up for a thousand and one different things in my life, but one of them will never be selling my soul to the devil.

You Can't Prove Love

Yesterday's Faustian Bargain highlighted the problems that arise when we sell our souls to the devil in order to get what we think we want. And often it's exactly that: what we *think* we want. All the babble that goes on in our heads convinces us that our life is second-rate and could be so much better. We dream of a bigger car, a better house, more time off and extensive world travel. We start to question the contribution those around us are making to that dream and that's when the rot sets in. It's always someone else's fault that we aren't where we want to be. Ultimately, we think by swapping our long-term partner for a new version who has more money and more get-up-and-go, we'll have solved all our problems.

It's never as simple as that and all the trinkets in the world won't replace basic love and loyalty. The moral of the Faustian story is that you always end up losing more than you hoped to gain. If you abandon those who *truly* love you in the pursuit of avarice, you will pay the terrible price of self-loathing. You can't possibly go through life running roughshod over everyone who gets in your way without leaving a trail of personal guilt behind. Other people do matter and our dealings with them shape who we are. Selfishness is the biggest destroyer of relationships going.

However, selfishness creeps up on us without us even being aware that it's there. It's a cunning little bugger. We get consumed by our own self-importance and imagine that we are a paradigm of virtue and generosity. In our mind, we catalogue all the good deeds we've done and compare them to those around us. We lose no opportunity to remind people of our generosity and how hard we work to make their lives better. Each repetition reinforces the inflated opinion we have of ourselves. It doesn't take long before we're full-blown narcissists. Sadly, in the midst of this blaze of self-aggrandisement, we often miss all the amazing things the wonderful people around us are doing. Just because they don't blow their own trumpet, doesn't mean they don't deserve significant fanfare.

My former mother-in-law illustrates a prime example of this sort of narcissism. Her ultimate retort to her only daughter, when she felt she wasn't getting the attention she thought she deserved, was: 'You have to prove to me that you love me.' Nobody should have to 'prove' love. You either experience it or you don't. It isn't a mathematical equation: 2+2=4. Fancy birthday presents+ fancy birthday presents=love. It is kindness and compassion, respect and understanding and most importantly, absolutely nothing to do with control. Trying to control someone financially or through emotional blackmail is not love, it's bullying. True love is doing something for someone because you want to, not because you think you then have control over them. You can't blackmail someone into loving you. You can't bribe someone into loving you. Love is something you give freely, with no strings attached.

The trouble with having power over someone else—be it financial or intellectual—is that it's so open to abuse. The one with power becomes egotistical and the one being bullied loses all sense of self-respect. It's a recipe for disaster in any relationship, but particularly, in any personal relationship. As we have seen, love can't be bought or brought about by bribery, it's something that comes from mutual respect. We need to respect those closest to us and appreciate all of their qualities; qualities that can be easily overlooked if we choose a Faustian bargain.

The moral of this story is that if we expect the one we love to 'prove' they love us, we actually don't love them, we love ourselves. If we don't know they love us instinctively, we perhaps should first look within ourselves to find out why. Even if deep down they do love us, nobody will find it easy to love a bully and no one will emit the non-verbal signals that make it official.

Compassion

On my walk yesterday, I was thinking about all my recent entries and feeling a bit guilty about my approach. I should be the last person to offer advice because I managed to get myself in a position where my ex decided to choose someone else over me after we'd spent a long period of time together. I'm hardly a paragon of virtue. But to be fair, I am only trying to encourage us all to look at a failed relationship objectively and find a few techniques to get over it. In a sense, this diary is about being betrayed, not about betraying, so that's my justification. However, if it was the other way around, I wonder if I'd even need to write a diary.

I think this somewhat rhetorical question gets to the nub of the matter. I am still struggling to understand what happened and although it's long done and dusted, I continue to search for ways to come to terms with the situation. The longer I search, the easier it gets. I'm not sure how my ex made her decision, but once she did, she wouldn't go back on it despite my willingness to forgive her. With hindsight, maybe she realised I wasn't the sort of man who could ever truly forgive her and perhaps she was right. In which case, I was the master of my own fate. During the course of our long relationship, we did talk about fidelity and both agreed it was sacrosanct. She said she would leave me if I cheated on her and I agreed I would probably do the same. But when it came to the crunch, I didn't want to sacrifice 24 years of my life with her for the sake of one mistake. We all make mistakes and some of them are pretty major ones. What I couldn't understand was her reluctance to acknowledge what she had done and was continuing to do. Moreover, I couldn't understand how she was expecting me to take responsibility for what she had done.

I pleaded with her to stop seeing her new man and try to save our marriage. I also told her how much I loved her regardless of what had happened. I was desperate to make things work even though she had been unfaithful and lied to me on numerous occasions. But she just wouldn't stop her affair. There was no hope for reconciliation if she wasn't prepared to be free of another involvement. You can't repair something involving two people when there is a third person in the picture. It's ridiculous and disgusting. To be honest, I think she made up her mind the moment she betrayed me. After that, it was a matter of justifying her actions in her own mind in order to release herself from guilt. Thinking back to those times when she humiliated me left, right and centre, that seems to be the only explanation. She hated herself because no matter what she threw at me, I still loved her. She hated herself because she was the only person who could fix the situation and yet she wasn't prepared to without losing face. She hated herself because she had broken the heart of a man who had been unerringly loyal to her and who had always been her champion. She hated herself because she had become the kind of person she actually abhorred. She hated herself because deep down she knew she had sold her soul to the devil.

I think when you have that amount of stuff to deal with, you've got to be incredibly strong. You have to be so strong that you can switch off any compassionate side to your nature and plough on regardless. You need to have the ability to reconcile your actions in whatever way you can. You need to be able to lie to yourself and everyone around you in order to survive. Sadly, you need to assume the persona of someone who isn't really you, and that is the tragic part of it all.

I think part of my own anguish in this whole sorry event is the realisation that the wonderful, kind and generous woman that I married has gone forever. She has destroyed herself from within. I find that as difficult to come to terms with as my own secondary problems. I hope she has some pretty robust burying techniques too.

The Meaning of Life

It's another one of those middle-of-the-night writing sessions. I had this rather confusing dream and woke myself up fighting off something or other. It wasn't anything too traumatic, so I didn't have a pounding heart or any particular anxiety, but it was enough to disturb my slumber. Once awake, however, the inevitable internal chatter started. My thoughts drifted from things that make me unhappy to things that make me happy and at that point, it was time to get up and write some of them down.

The older I get, the less I seem to understand the meaning of life. The classic Monty Python film didn't help to clear things up for me either. All I can remember from The Meaning of Life are the sketches about Mr Creosote and the one involving the song 'Every Sperm is Sacred.' One is disgusting—but also incredibly funny—and the other pokes fun at all manner of institutions. Perhaps none of us can comprehend the meaning of life, so we use humour to distract us along the way. I certainly think humour is one of the things that makes me happy and helps me navigate life. One of the amazing things about humour is its ability to diffuse tension. By diffusing tension, it concurrently breaks down barriers and consequentially becomes the vehicle for truth. Shakespeare's fool got away with blue murder, and in King Lear, he acted as the King's conscience and through irony, sarcasm and humour, he was able to point out Lear's faults. I like the idea of humour being a vehicle for truth.

You can also introduce the wildest concepts under the guise of 'I'm only joking' and can even get away with pointing out everyone's fallibility by using self-deprecating humour. People can recognise their own weaknesses in you and relate to them in a non-threatening way. Like alcohol, humour often softens the edges and oils the wheels of self-discovery. It allows us to think outside the box, challenge dogma and liberate our minds. It's one of life's real detoxing agents. By keeping our spirits up, it can have amazing physical benefits. I'm definitely a fan of humour.

So, what else makes me happy? Well, there are lots of things. In a world of conformity, nature is a breath of fresh air. I enjoy seeing birds going about their daily lives almost oblivious to us. They sing when they want to, they build nests when they want to, and they crap on our newly washed cars when they want to. Their independence makes me happy. In fact, anything in life that does its own thing unfettered by human intervention makes me happy. Watching the choreography of clouds or the motion of the sea makes me happy. Witnessing anything grow. Gazing up at the stars liberates my soul and makes me realise how inconsequential we all are in the great scheme of things. Freedom makes me happy.

I think these last couple of points could be the moral of today's story. Our lives are an infinitesimally small part of what goes on here on Earth, let alone the universe. In the briefest moments we've been allotted, we should be sure to make the most of them. Life may be a mystery, but it's a spectacular mystery that we are very privileged to enjoy.

Abandonment

When I woke up this morning, I experienced one of those feelings of nervousness that have plagued me for the last 32 months. It was essentially a panic attack and I'm not sure I've identified its genesis before now. A few entries ago, I talked about the American legal drama, Suits and this TV programme has remained my regular viewing diet ever since. Not only does the lead character Harvey have a hang-up about his mother cheating on his father, but he has even bigger abandonment issues. I've realised my panic attacks are much like his and they are brought on by exactly the same feelings.

In the course of a long-lasting relationship, you learn to trust your partner. Your lives become inseparable and you rely on each other for emotional support and backing in every other aspect of your partnership. You learn to trust them in the same way you trust your parents in a normal healthy family unit. Indeed, the reason most of us grow up to be confident and well-balanced adults is rooted in those early years of security. If that carpet of emotional stability is suddenly ripped out from under you, it can be devastating. I was very fortunate not to have that happen to me in childhood, but—as they would say in Suits—it sure as hell happened to me as an adult.

After both my parents passed away, my life revolved around my ex and she became my number-one go-to. I trusted that she would be there for me in every conceivable situation, and likewise, I would be there for her as well. It is the foundation that all good, healthy relationships are built on. When the bombshell hit and it became obvious my ex had found someone else, it really was devastating. The sense of abandonment was palpable. My whole life became unstuck and all the security nets that allowed me to lead an emotionally stable life were suddenly gone. My number one confidant and soul mate had dumped me.

It's quite an eye-opener looking back on all of this after 32 months as it makes me realise how deep the scars continue to run. Subconsciously, I am still feeling vulnerable and even though the morning panic attacks are much less severe than they used to be, I haven't quite put things to rest just yet. However, realistically I have nothing to worry about. I am in a wonderful new relationship and I trust my partner implicitly. She is kind, caring and amazingly loyal and supportive. She has seen me wrestle with a kaleidoscope of emotions that have almost torn me apart. She has been by my side through thick and thin and gently guided me along the road to recovery. I have said this before and I'll say it again, I'm a very lucky man.

As I continue to negotiate this traumatic experience with the love and support of my new partner, I am mindful of all the people in the world who have faced similar devastating feelings of abandonment. These wounds take a long time to heal and the only ointment that speeds up the recovery process is love. Since love and trust share a symbiotic relationship, I am confident my ongoing therapy will win the day.

Grey Areas

I'm a little late starting my entry this morning as I had a lot on my mind during the night. We had a late-night visitor with some important news, so it was a lot to process. It's amazing how active the mind can be at such an inconvenient time! Not to worry, I'm getting better at making decisions these days and I'm happy to leave things in the lap of the gods.

Nothing in life is certain and all we can ever do is make decisions based on the information we have to hand. Most of the time, the results are completely out of our control. Learning to deal with possible disappointments is one of our biggest learning curves. I've spent so much of my life worrying about the decisions I've made and beating myself up when they didn't turn out the way that I'd planned. It's such a silly exercise and a very destructive process. If we live our lives second-guessing everything we do, we'll eventually end up powerless.

Constantly thinking back on a failed relationship that wasn't instigated by us, is another form of second-guessing; we're just rehashing something that was completely out of our control. It becomes a self-inflicted torture that never ends. It also stops us from moving forward with our lives because we're afraid it might happen all over again. But the reality is, we didn't make any mistakes and there was nothing we could possibly have done differently based on the circumstances we found ourselves in. Realising that we were powerless to change things then, makes us powerful now.

I'm only talking about our own internal power struggles and nothing to do with exerting power over other people which smacks of narcissism. Having a strong internal power to make decisions and to stick by them makes life so much easier. It presupposes we have the strength to overcome any setbacks and creates the kind of liberating environment that fosters confidence in ourselves. Often a relationship breakdown knocks our confidence levels for six and it can take years to build them up again. But, bit by bit, we can become whole again. We've just got to start trusting ourselves and the decisions we make. Life is never black and white; we need to accept and be comfortable with the grey areas as well.

Honesty

Moments of weakness come and go. Life tends to be a series of ups and downs and when we're up, we're very, very up, and when we're down…well, we're down. In fact—and continuing this morning's nursery rhyme theme—I often feel like the Grand Old Duke of York, marching my ten thousand emotions up to the top of the hill and then marching them down again. I wonder if everyone experiences life in the same way, or are some people more consistently optimistic?

I guess life is about contrasts. It's about good and evil, black and white, hot and cold, dark and light, happy and sad. Without each opposing characteristic, things would be bland. Constant daylight would become tiring, just as much as living in the dark all the time would make us a bit depressed. Likewise, it's impossible to be happy all of the time, because you can't really appreciate how happy you are until you feel some sadness. In order to function successfully as human beings, we actually need some ups and downs.

Balancing these mood swings is the important thing. If we are prone to massive variations in temperament, things can get a bit complicated. Bipolar disorder is an example of extreme mood swings that can impact on a person's life and those around them. Living with such a condition must be very challenging for everyone concerned. But even if we are lucky enough to avoid such a medical state, day-to-day mood swings can take their toll. How do we stop ourselves falling into these unstable mental states? For me, it's been an ongoing voyage of discovery and I'm pretty sure, this is the case for most people. Like me, some people are happy to admit it, others, on the other hand, hide any trace of weakness to the world. On the whole, I think it is much better to be open and honest about our mental state, without getting too hung up with it in the process. Much better to get things out in the open rather than bottle them up and implode. Extreme depression is often the result of such bottling up. Even supposedly relatively well-balanced people can come to grief if they don't find some form of outlet for their frustrations. Frustration and depression are very closely linked.

We all get frustrated when we can't seem to solve a problem or if things just don't seem to be going our way. It's Sod's law. Nothing we do appears to alleviate the situation and we end up feeling trapped and useless. Banging our head against a brick wall is very debilitating and doing it enough times drags us into one of those inevitable downward turns. The trick is to try to break the cycle before it even has a chance to get hold of us. Don't bottle it up, share it. Use humour to soften the delivery and find someone who is happy to help diffuse the situation before it gets out of hand. Be open and honest and don't worry about 'losing face.' There is no such thing. A fake persona makes a fake person and no one wants to deal with one of those. You can't help someone who lies to you and you can't be helped yourself if you aren't honest about how you feel.

The answer then to keeping our lives on a more even keel, is honesty. Being honest with ourselves and those around us. There will always be ups and downs in the course of our lives, but they won't be as extreme or debilitating if we have a good honesty escape valve.

Revenge

Rebuilding ourselves after the devastation of heartbreak is one of the biggest challenges we can face in life. It involves restoring so many complicated and interrelated strands that it is difficult to know where to start. From my personal experience, there doesn't seem to be any quick fix either and I even wonder whether we can truly 'fix' things anyway. I know all this sounds rather fatalistic, but I'm determined to be honest in this diary and as I mentioned yesterday, honesty is often the best policy. However, although we may not be able to fix things, we should be able to find a way to live with them.

I think in the course of over 60 entries in this diary, I've discussed the whole gamut of heartbreak emotions and their related feelings. They include regret, anger, abandonment, self-pity, resentment, loathing and betrayal. But one aspect I haven't touched on is revenge. Now, you may be wondering how on earth revenge could be an emotion to discuss constructively in the course of this sort of recovery process, but it does have a role to play. I think it probably has a role to play pre-breakup too.

The lead-up to any failed relationship that involves one party leaving the other and committing adultery, must be driven by a sense of frustration and feelings of being let down. They resent their partner for not being the person they want them to be and therefore strive to prove to themselves and to the world that they are right. They harbour so much resentment that the very act of betrayal becomes a form of revenge. They only feel totally justified when they have established the new perfect relationship they always wanted and can tell the world how the end justified the means. This is their perfect revenge and allows them to move forward with their lives. If things were only so simple.

Cheating on someone you love, or at least loved, as a form of revenge for perceived weaknesses, is abominable. It requires a very twisted mindset. Life is full of temptations and if we gave into all of them, we'd be a mess, as would everyone around us. Any form of revenge always turns out badly. It doesn't fix anything; it just perpetuates injustices. We just need to think of Shakespeare's Othello. Often the perceived injustices we feel turn out to be unfounded and the resultant revenge hollow, if not tragic.

For the person that has been betrayed, revenge of any sort is equally pointless. Life is too short to hold grudges and the best way for everyone is to move forward. Someone eventually needs to be the bigger person and not perpetuate a tragic cycle.

New Regime

Greetings, world! I woke up this morning with the age-old feelings of sickness in my stomach and anxiety. I often wonder if I'll ever be the same again after the last two and a half years of emotional torture. Unfortunately, old habits die hard and I find myself slipping back into them so easily. All it takes is a stray thought which I follow through on and I'm away to that very familiar self-torture zone. Am I the only weak person in the world still struggling with betrayal and heartbreak, years after the event? Probably not, but that's no consolation.

I find I'm more likely to return to these dark zones when I'm tired or hungover. Somehow the ability to block out unwelcome thoughts becomes harder in either state. It's as if cognitive weakness allows our emotions free access to our minds. It's certainly clinically proven that our emotions have more sway over the thinking part of the mind rather than the other way around. Hence, everyone struggles to keep negative emotions at bay. The logical solution would be to remain sober and get lots of sleep. If only we were all capable of instigating the logical solution!

But even if we are in a somewhat compromised state, the battle continues. To avoid those dreaded demons taking hold, our coping systems need to be automated. This requires day-to-day training over a long period of time. We need to set up an impenetrable defence system that allows for the inevitable periodic cognitive meltdown. When I first started writing this diary, I was fired up by blocking techniques and I practised them consistently for a month. The results were amazing. My mood swings levelled out and I almost became a different person. By blocking out all thoughts of my painful relationship failure and anything to do with my ex, life became exciting again. I also gained a new sense of purpose.

The answer then is consistency and having the resolve to start all over again when necessary. I am at this point now. In the last few weeks, I've found myself slipping back into old bad habits and it's time to reboot and reform those neural pathways that lead to a healthier mental state devoid of regret, anger, guilt, longing and self-incrimination. It's all very well writing about as many positive things as possible every day, but without actually implementing the fundamentals of mental recovery, it's merely an academic exercise and pointless. No one said getting over heartbreak would be easy, it just requires a plan and one that we must stick to. Everything in life is a matter of two steps forward and one step back and as long as we have the resolve to keep moving forward, we can overcome anything. My resolve starts again now. Any time one of those destructive thoughts pops into my mind, I'm going to block it and think of something completely different and uplifting. I have two choices: To sink or to swim. I'm choosing to swim. Let the new regime begin!

Worry

I've been reading a book about worry in the last few days and I thought it might be an idea to chew the cud with this topic today. Some of us seem to be born worriers and others have the ability just to get on with life. I think I'm probably in the former category, although I've possibly hovered between the two states in various periods of my life. Worry has a great bearing on the way we deal with any traumatic period in our lives. If you are like me, you end up worrying about every aspect of your life at the expense of actually living it.

This diary is all about coming to terms with heartbreak and the distressing times associated with it. When the most important person in your life exits from it, you worry about how you are going to cope in the big wide world on your own. You worry about ever finding someone like her/him ever again. You worry about losing all your friends and you worry about being heartbroken forever. These worries are very real at the time and increase the stress levels in an already stressful situation. But worry, like many emotions, is largely self-induced and self-perpetuating. It makes mountains out of molehills and provides little or no genuine benefit to a stressful situation. It's almost as if it has become a requirement for dealing with any difficult situation and without it, there is no way to move forward. Unfortunately, what starts out as rumination soon escalates into catastrophising. Of course, it's a quite natural symptom of our world being turned upside down. However, by worrying about everything, we are simply exacerbating the situation and not solving anything.

It's time to debunk the worry myth. Worry doesn't achieve anything tangible; actions do. Worry is a form of overthinking that actually short-circuits the mind. There are so many synapses firing, the poor old brain almost starts to smoke. Every single mild negative thought is blown out of all proportion and ends up as a catastrophe. What started out as an innocent, but quite a pertinent question: 'Will I ever find anyone else?' ends up becoming 'There is no one else in the world like him/her, so I am going to die alone with a broken heart.' The process of getting from the first question to the latter answer becomes a harrowing journey of epic proportions. It's pointless and very self-destructive.

In the course of my journey of self-rehabilitation, I have discovered one thing for sure: we are often our own worst enemies. We torture ourselves with thoughts that have no basis in reality or fact. We make up scenarios that are largely fiction. Even if there is a strand of truth in our fairy tale, we'll distort it into some hideous misrepresentation of the real situation. We seem to be on a reckless course towards self-annihilation. Worry is one of the many tools we use for self-destruction.

It's a terrible indictment to the human race that things have got so bad. We might have clawed our way to the top of the food chain, but having got there, we are hell-bent on destroying ourselves from within. Tragic or what? Now of course, this is an exaggeration of the state of play for homo sapiens at this point in time, but it does illustrate quite nicely how we can catastrophise anything if we have a mind to. And yes, almost everything is in the mind. We are masters of our own destiny only if we master our minds. We must be constantly searching for ways to tame the wild beast that rages within us. We must constantly remind ourselves that our primordial instincts are out of place in modern society. The fact is, we're most unlikely to be eaten by a tiger on the way to the supermarket. We might get run over by a food trolley or get our Toyota bashed in the carpark, but that's probably the worst it gets. If the manager of the butchery department was prone to attacking his customers with a meat cleaver, we might actually have something to worry about. We shouldn't worry about things that have very little chance of ever happening. We should give ourselves a good talking to and show who's the boss. Superstitions and bad mental habits shouldn't be in the driving seat and if we let our emotions rule the roost, we'll probably end up worrying ourselves sick.

The Hidden Enemy

If only everyone in the world would follow a code of openness and honesty, our lives would be enhanced immeasurably. Trust would be *de rigueur* and we could all go about our daily lives in safety and harmony. Sadly, this rather naive idea can never take traction because there will always be people who want to be better than other people. There will always be people who want to be successful on the backs of other people and there will always be people who only feel worthy when they are belittling other people. It's a terrible reflection on society that such skulduggery still exists and moreover, is allowed to exist.

Don't get me wrong, I think on a scale of one to ten, our society is generally hitting a good six. We aren't living in the Wild West with gun-slingers on every street corner or bandits ambushing us on the way to the shops. But unfortunately, these murderers and terrorists have simply gone underground and are operating subversively. All the basic instincts of greed and self-aggrandisement are achieved with twenty-first-century weapons that don't involve firearms or clubs. Bullies have much more subtle forms of murder and extortion. Twenty-first-century crimes have increasingly become psychological rather than physical. People are being destroyed from within by mental torture and the resultant stress-related diseases associated with such underhand tactics. Today's gun-slingers are contract killers of a different kind. They are not contracted to kill; the contracts are killing. No matter where you turn, there will be a contract to sign. Sign up for a mortgage, sign up for a credit card, sign up for a job, sign up for funeral cover, sign up for a therapist, sign up for a vaccine. Sign up for your right to live in the society that has been created for you. If you don't sign up and follow all the rules, you're out. And if you are naive enough to miss all the fine print, there's a nasty sting in the tail waiting for you, just when you don't need it.

Of course, on the surface, everything is very civilised. We go about our daily lives being superficially nice to each other and to a certain extent, there is even a sense of camaraderie as we duly sign on the dotted line and collectively moan about bureaucracy. But whether we like it or not, we'll eventually have to face a gun-slinger or bandit if we have the audacity to step out of line. Even if we try to be Mr or Mrs Goody Two-shoes, the work bully will see an opening and pounce on us. Like any predator, they pick off the weakest members of the herd. All of this leads to frightening levels of psychological stress that are knocking off decent, honest and open people at an alarming rate. The mental health service can't cope and countless people end up falling through the cracks.

I know I'm painting a very dark picture of the world today, but we can survive if we can learn some techniques to combat these hidden enemies. Everything can be reduced to personal relationships and if we can find a way to circumvent a bully one-on-one, we'll be better able to circumvent a collective, bureaucratic bully. Don't let them get to you. Don't let them place the seeds of doubt that grow into seeds of self-destruction. Don't let them slip you a mental virus that will eventually eat you up.

I've learnt a lot about coping with heartbreak and manipulation in a personal relationship and these tools and techniques will ameliorate other aspects of my life too. We may have faced the biggest challenge in our lives surviving our stay in Heartbreak Hotel, but we will definitely come out a stronger person in the end.

Legacy

In the course of our time on earth, we touch so many people's lives, even if we don't really realise it. Interacting with other people is one of the most important things we do. It's a great privilege, but it's also a great responsibility. Building trust is one of the biggest parts of it and this can happen over a long period of time or in the course of just a few encounters. Long-lasting relationships are the most valuable of course because getting to know someone intimately takes a lot of time and the trust we then share is on a completely different level. That's why, wham, bam and off-you-go one-night stands must be so unsatisfactory. Having never indulged in such things myself, I can't speak from personal experience, but I can imagine they must leave you feeling pretty emotionally empty. There is something really special about long-lasting personal friendships which involve varying degrees of emotional involvement.

Our emotions are such a big driving force in whatever we do. All our close personal friendships have to contain them because that's what constitutes love. We can meet someone new and instantly like them—because they share our way of thinking and lots of common interests—but it takes months or years for that mutual attraction to turn into something much deeper. Love, at first sight, is probably impossible since physical attraction is only a very small part of the chemistry required to form a lasting bond. In terms of a platonic relationship or any relationship that will never be anything more than friendship, physical attraction has nothing to do with the equation anyway. Love is indeed a many-splendored thing.

The process of moving from liking to loving is usually long and complicated and as we've seen, it involves different things for different forms of relationships. Platonic love, or love of friends, not partners, is of course based on trust and understanding and a growing concern for their wellbeing. We want them to be happy and we want them to lead safe and worthwhile lives. We want to be a part of their successes and be there for them in difficult times. You can trust friends with personal details and seek their advice, but you probably wouldn't ask them to sacrifice anything on your behalf. The love of a partner is different and much more intense. Of course, it contains all the facets that friendship does—so it is a form of friendship—but it is so much more. It's an all-consuming commitment to someone else, with an unwavering undertaking to honour and look after one another through thick and thin. It's the most magical engagement we can have in our lives and one that should be cherished. To a certain extent, friends can come and go because our lives are fluid and we often need to change jobs and relocate. But partnerships are different, and so they should be. We move with the person we love, or they move with us. There is never any question about this and the need for negotiation is minimal, so deep runs the course of true love.

The breakdown of true love is indescribably hard to deal with since it encapsulates often decades of emotional interactions. You invest so much emotional energy in the other person and build a mutually dependent life together. You imagine you know how your partner thinks and can almost predict their next move in most situations. Ultimately, they become an extension of you. It is a very precious coupling of two souls in a mad, mad world. Then suddenly, often out of nowhere, your most precious creation crumbles before your eyes. The person who has been an integral part of you for so many years breaks that magical bond and dumps you. Devastation ensues and the long road to recovery begins.

If you are like me, you value everyone you meet in life. You try to see the good in them and want to help them in any way you can. In that respect, it's our legacy to this world. Of course, there will be people we don't 'click' with and they are best avoided after we've done our best to understand them. But for the people we do relate to, our interactions are priceless. Part of us lives on in them and them in us. They help to make us who we are and we help to make them who they are. It's a great responsibility on both sides and one we shouldn't take lightly. I don't have masses of friends for that very reason; you simply can't look after a multitude of people with that sort of care and attention.

Even when things ultimately go wrong, I'm proud of my approach and I wouldn't lead my life in any other way. I invested everything in my 24-year relationship with my ex. She was my constant and unwavering focus throughout the whole time. She meant everything to me and I thought I meant everything to her. We'd experienced so much and overcome every imaginable hurdle on our way through our great journey together. But it wasn't to be and she decided she needed to explore a new journey with a different person. I'm still glad I was loyal, honest and devoted to her for all those years because that's who I am. I'm sure I wasn't the best husband in a lot of ways, but I never compromised on those core values.

My recovery process is continuing on a daily basis and the more I think about this heartbreaking journey, the more I begin to understand who I am. In fact, the more I understand what should be my priorities in life. Despite everything that has happened, I will always remain loyal to my friends and be open and honest with them. I just need to constantly remind myself that whether I like it or not, my interactions with them will become an integral part of who they are and who they become. Likewise with my new partner, who is now my ultimate friend. It is one of life's great responsibilities, to take care of the people we meet. Treat everyone with care and respect because your interactions with them will be indelibly imprinted on them forever. We should bless people's lives with our presence, not damage them. If there is any more worthwhile legacy to leave, I can't think of it.

The 'Genuine' Radar

Yesterday, I explored the possibility that our greatest legacy is the influence we have on the people we meet during the course of our lives and encouraging us all to make that a positive, rather than a negative outcome. It seems a pretty straightforward objective, but it's so easy to get sucked into taking a defensive stance with whomever we meet and doubting their integrity. The big wide world trains us to be suspicious, because suspicion keeps us safe from unscrupulous people. We hear countless stories of rip-off artists conning large amounts of money out of unsuspecting victims. We are constantly on our guard against the dodgy car dealer or investment broker who doesn't think twice about taking our hard-earned cash. Life is full of sharks, so why should we let our defences down and make ourselves open to having our arm and a leg bitten off?

The trouble with such generalised thinking is that it presupposes guilt, until proven innocent. It doesn't take into account that at least 90% of the population is honest and trustworthy. It perpetuates a society of negativity and doesn't celebrate the freedoms and communal trust that we are so lucky to share. It creates people who are always on their back foot looking to be betrayed. Sadly, scaremongering has become big business and countless people fall for it hook, line, and sinker.

If we are to avoid being swallowed up by this negative quicksand, maybe our best bet is to treat everyone at face value and try to see the good in them rather than suspecting something untoward at the outset. If we treat people the way we would like to be treated ourselves, perhaps the world would be a better place. I'm often surprised at the number of seemingly miserable-looking people who will break into a wonderfully warm smile if I smile first. People who are initially very much on the defensive can melt like butter with some genuine encouragement and interest in their lives. We all blossom when someone shows genuine interest in us and our story. The flip side to this hinges on the word *genuine*.

How often have you met someone who initially asks you polite questions concerning who you are and what you do, only to turn everything back to themselves without even waiting for a reply? They bulldoze their way through their interaction with you without displaying the slightest bit of empathy or caring a toss about your feelings. Even if you do manage to get a word in edgeways, that word will be ridiculed and tossed aside. You leave the encounter with a sense of disbelief and feelings of annihilation. It's as if your whole being has been crushed to smithereens. Quite frankly, people like that need to be avoided. The kindest thing to do—but that's never our initial reaction having met them—is to put them down (probably the best option!) as misguided, or suffering from some affliction that is beyond our control, and just move on. Unfortunately, narcissists will never leave a positive legacy because they are incapable of comprehending the needs of the people around them. They are devoid of genuine understanding and have no empathy towards their fellow man. So much of this arises out of emotional insecurity. They bulldoze to camouflage their biggest weakness: a complete inability to read and interpret other people's emotions.

Thankfully, it doesn't take too long to spot a bully as they are so full of their own self-importance that they won't be even willing to give you the time of day. What we need to do is develop a radar for genuine, like-minded people and then our mutual legacy can begin.

Regardless of whom we meet on our journey through life, I think it's important to give everyone the benefit of the doubt, to begin with. Even superficially grumpy people can turn out to have hearts of gold. Genuine friendship, like Rome, wasn't built in a day. It's a process that can take a considerable amount of time, moving from one level of trust to the next almost imperceptibly. Fortunately, the real sharks and manipulators are rare, so our legacies are achievable if we only remain open and keep our radar well-tuned.

Let It Go

I am painfully aware that the scars from my broken marriage are going to be with me for the rest of my life. The failure of this relationship has turned my world upside down, had a profound effect on me, and changed the course of my life dramatically. It has been a heartbreaking and gut-wrenching experience that I wouldn't want anyone to go through. In this diary, I've tried to catalogue some of the myriad feelings that have coursed through me over the last two and three-quarter years as I try to come to terms with something I will probably never come to terms with.

For some reason, I never expected to be faced with such a life-changing scenario. I had sailed through life nonchalantly, presupposing the calm waters would continue. Okay, there had been a few choppy periods, as people very close to me exited my world through natural causes, but on the whole, the effects of such losses were relatively short-lived, at least on a superficial level. When people close to you die, the pain is real and biting, but there is an inevitability about it that can't be challenged; you simply can't bring them back no matter how much you try. It's a very painful resolution, but a kind of resolution nonetheless.

Unless suicide is involved, there are also no feelings of deliberate abandonment. People who leave us in these situations don't do so because they want to, they leave us because their days are numbered and it's out of their control. The love we felt for them is 'oft interred with their bones' to use a marvellous Shakespearian phrase. But the love we still feel for them is undoubtedly interred in our bones and will be for the rest of our lives. On the other hand, when betrayal is involved, our love has nowhere to go. It floats about in an endless vacuum, spurned and degraded beyond belief, finding no solace or resting place. It's a cruel, eternal prison sentence for one of life's magical and unsuspecting creations and its ether haunts us for the rest of our days, if we let it.

Therefore, to betray someone's love is probably one of the cruellest things anyone can do. It leaves no room for resolution and leaves the heartbroken person grappling with their emotions for the remainder of their days. It's hard to imagine what motivates such wanton disregard for another person's feelings. Of course, I'm not talking about superficial love, the kind of love many people experience on the road to a long-lasting, full-blown relationship. Those kinds of flings end more in disappointment rather than earth-shattering heartbreak. The recovery process is often relatively short and doesn't leave too many scars. But betrayal on the grandest scale, after decades together, is a different scenario. The scars seldom heal and the experience has life-long repercussions.

For those of us on the receiving end of such emotional vandalism, retaining our integrity is paramount. We need to find tangible ways of letting our unrequited love go. We have to let it go to endure its cruel fate, but let it go, we must. Yes, our lives have changed, and yes, they will never be the same again. But no, we don't need to end up in the same vacuum. Cut the string and let it go.

Decisions

Yesterday, I talked about letting go and the need to move on from heartbreak and its attendant emotions. But life in general is all about moving on and having the courage to put things behind us. The stronger we grow, the greater ability we have to make decisions and stick by them. So often we spend enormous amounts of time second-guessing our decisions and doubting our ability to make them effectively. We end up living in limbo land where there is no going forward and certainly no going back.

As I grow stronger, the more I realise that the ability to move forward is what makes the difference between happy and contented people and miserable and disgruntled people. Each group suffers the same setbacks in life, but they deal with them differently. The happy and contented people are always looking for the good in a situation, the disgruntled ones, the bad. So actually, the decisions we make are really immaterial, but the way we react to the results of our decisions is paramount. Everything in life requires us to make a decision: We need to decide to get up in the morning or stay in bed. We need to decide to have tea or coffee for breakfast. We need to decide whether to buy a new car or stick with the old one.

It's not always us making the decisions either. Some people decide to dump their partner and find a new one. Other people's decisions can be thrust upon us and they're not always to our liking. But once again, it's how we *react* that's important, not the decision itself. My relationship breakup experience over the last two and three-quarter years has taught me a lot about how I react. My wife's decision to move on after 24 years produced an automated reaction of devastation. I was in a negative mindset that was only capable of that response. After years of psychological abuse, not only was I incapable of making decisions myself, but I also couldn't react in a constructive way to other people's decisions that were about to impact on me in such a decisive manner. I was a decision wreck.

With hindsight, I could have handled things a lot better if I'd only discovered what I know today: It's not the decisions we make, or the decisions that are made for us that matter, it's how we react to them. It's taken me two and three-quarter years to discover this secret, but two and three-quarter years well spent. If we learn to react positively to everything that we experience in life and always move forward, not backwards, we will never be phased by anything. Every imaginable catastrophe in life always has a flip side if we view it as a learning experience and make the decision to move on. Reacting to our own decisions and those around us with a positive mindset can transform our lives from purgatory to heaven in the blink of an eye. There is no such thing as a bad decision, only an unhelpful reaction.

Mountains out of Molehills

Stress is probably one of the world's biggest killers. It's an insidious bugger that wreaks havoc on your nervous system and eventually most other parts of your body too. Hypertension, one of its common outcomes, is aptly called a silent killer since if you don't have regular blood pressure checks, it can finish you off without you even knowing about it. Scary stuff. There are lots of things in life that can finish us off without us even knowing it. Our world is full of silent killers and we need to be on our guard to identify them before they can do their dirty deeds.

Any situation that makes us feel trapped is a cause for concern because without an escape route, the tension rises and the stress levels with it. Stress is always the result of backing ourselves into a corner. And I say 'ourselves' with good reason. Almost everyone has an amazing ability to make mountains out of molehills, it's as if it's programmed into our DNA. The bigger the mountains become, the higher up the stress scale we go. It's also uncanny the way one stressful situation gives rise to another almost exponentially. When you're late for work, you can almost guarantee the car won't start, and then when it does and you're halfway down the street, you'll suddenly remember you didn't pick up that important document you need for the day. Sod's law or what? Having a 'bad day' is so true, because it almost invariably goes from bad to worse in a very short space of time. Now, it's fanciful to imagine there is some mystical 'bad day' being up in the sky coordinating all our mayhem, but realistically, it's just us and a build-up of self-generated stress. We've amplified tiny little triggers over a period of time until our stress levels are out of control and no matter what we do, there will be stress associated with it. Fortunately, with most everyday stress, there comes a popping point. Everything escalates to such a high degree that the only way out is to pop, and when we do, it's such a relief.

If we can only identify these little triggers and diffuse them before they get out of hand, our lives will be much more peaceful and probably last a lot longer.

Much of this diffusing occurs when we realise that most of life's challenges are molehills, not mountains; everyday niggles that are not of any earth-shattering consequence. Stepping back and trying to see the big picture helps enormously. In terms of failed relationships, it's realising that there are, indeed, 'plenty of fish in the sea.' When one door closes, another eventually opens as long as we don't get swamped by the details around us. I for one, spent far too much time wallowing in self-pity and struggling to see any way out of the corner I found myself in. I convinced myself that my marriage was *the* most important thing in my life and without it, I was nothing. Having convinced myself of that, I didn't have any escape route and suffered accordingly. If I'd only been in a more encompassing mindset, I'd have realised that life never consists of just one chance at anything; we have multiple opportunities to get things right. 'One and only' thinking leads to entrapment and entrapment leads to corners we can't get out of. And corners we can't escape from lead to stress, and stress leads to more stress and more stress leads to illness and illness leads to death. Dying from a broken heart is perfectly feasible if we don't break this self-destructive cycle. We'll all end up in an early grave if we lose sight of the bigger picture and get bogged down in the minutia.

Let's go easy on ourselves and forget about those molehills. Instead, let's start scaling the mountains and begin to enjoy the amazing vistas from every peak we conquer.

Stereotypes

Interactions are always interesting. Last night, my partner and I visited our neighbours to celebrate a birthday, it was an enjoyable evening with an eclectic group of people. It got me thinking about how we all interacted and what lessons are to be learned.

I've often witnessed the classic couple dynamic which involves the man strutting about complaining about the woman not paying attention to what he says and having to do things just to keep her happy. And the woman making suggestions that if he did certain things, he would get more action in the bedroom department. It's such a stereotype and one that seems prevalent in today's society. Both are acting out their respective roles perfectly, but I wonder if such relationships have lost touch with what really matters. Surely, it should be a pleasure creating an environment that supports your partner, not a chore? Surely, intimacy should be a two-way thing, not something that is offered on special occasions? The more I think about it, the more I realise that we can spend our whole lives acting out parts in an incredible farce.

Now, I'm not for one moment suggesting that these couples aren't incredibly fond of each other and may well be in a very strong and long-lasting relationship, but I am suggesting that if we all ditched the stereotypes, we might live much more rewarding lives. I'm certainly over joining a male huddle that involves complaining about our partner's irrational behaviour and how we are always compromising to make things work. It's disrespectful to the person we love and has no intrinsic value. Likewise, my partner is over joining girly gatherings that end up as a moan-fest about the men in their lives. Really, what's the point? Is it gender solidarity or just assuming a role that society perpetuates? We for two, don't want a part of it.

But the trouble is, we all want to fit in, we want to be accepted and not become outcasts. But then the trouble is, it leads to a herd mentality that destroys our ability for independent thought. In fact, we end up doing things that are completely alien to our core values and eventually sell our souls to a collective devil. Some of the world's worst atrocities have happened for this very reason. It's not that all the individuals involved were intrinsically rotten, it's because the herd mentality took over and it became impossible to stop the ensuing stampede.

Fortunately, education has had a profoundly beneficial effect on the way society functions. It gives us the skills to question accepted authority and the knowledge to avoid repeating destructive behaviours. So, why then does the herd mentality still prevail? It's because bullies exist and their overpowering personalities have the ability to swamp reasonable behaviour. Think of any example of genocide and there will be a bully associated with it. There are even seemingly benevolent bullies who coerce us with their rhetoric. We get sucked in by their sweet talk and end up betraying those around us.

I guess the trick is to be discerning and avoid any situation that involves dominant personalities. Either that, or try to remain impartial. Fence sitting is much preferable to crowd-mongering. The problem with bullies is that they are never prepared to listen to an opposing view, they just want to steamroll over everyone around them. If we try to use the same tactics to turn them, we simply become like them. Opposition using the same tools perpetuates the injustice, it never countermands it. Gandhi could never have achieved what he did by using the tools of his oppressors. We can never challenge a bully by being one. Staying true to our core beliefs in the face of the gang mentality is one of the hardest things to do, but also the most rewarding. Conventions and stereotypes are just bullies in sheep's clothing and I personally want none of it.

Panic

When I first started writing this diary, I was still experiencing major repercussions from the failure of my marriage two and three-quarter years ago. My former wife haunted me in my dreams and haunted me in every thought I had during my waking moments. It was a cruel prison sentence with no parole. She had been my judge, jury and executioner rolled into one and I hadn't even committed a crime. In 24 years, I'd never cheated on her, in 24 years, I had always supported her in everything she did, and in 24 years, I had loved her unconditionally. But somewhere along the line, she decided that wasn't enough and dumped me for another man. It was a devastating thing to do to a person who had invested so much in the relationship and who had shown the kind of loyalty and trust some couples can only dream about. It was a bitter pill to swallow for sure.

But that was then and this is now. Eighty-three diary entries later and I'm a much stronger person. I can view the whole breakup objectively and even revisit parts of it without being thrown into a horrible state of depression. Of course, there are still triggers that cause flushes of regret and disappointment, but they are not the norm and depression is certainly not something I want to indulge in anymore. This transformation has occurred across the board in my life and isn't related solely to my marital woes. I am now dealing with life differently and trying to have a fair and balanced view of every situation that arises on a day-to-day basis. To put it simply, I'm trying to take the panic out of living.

When we are thrown into a seemingly impossible situation, our natural reaction is to panic. All reasonable thought goes out the window and we flap about not knowing what to do. In normal circumstances, such panic attacks only last for a limited period and until the danger is over. But in extreme cases—like the end of a long-term relationship—the panic can last for years. This was the situation I found myself in. My life as I knew it had come to an abrupt end and I had absolutely no idea how I was going to be able to carry on. Every morning, I woke up with feelings of panic and hopelessness. Every day, I was consumed by grief, regret, heartbreak and longing. It was a living hell that I just couldn't escape from.

I think everyone probably deals with these situations in a different way and their respective roads to recovery take different routes. Mine has most definitely involved self-therapy. Every day for eighty-one days, I have written an entry that tries to describe some aspects of the things I've been going through. They may have been inspired by a dream, or just a thought that had occurred during the course of the day. Early on, they catalogued my feelings of depression and panic and my attempts to block the appalling negative thoughts that inhabited my mind. Often, I lashed out in a vitriolic manner, consumed by anger and resentment at what had happened. Sometimes, I even tried to set a reconciliatory tone and diffuse the situation with ideas that fate had simply played its part and it was all out of my control. It really has been a rollercoaster of random thoughts and ideas attempting to make sense of the senseless. To understand the incomprehensible and to heal the incurable. However, whatever way this journey evolved, it evolved constructively. It has furnished that all-important escape route that we all need in order to recover. Alcohol, distractions and other people have played their part of course, but if we don't try to sort ourselves out from within, we'll never fully recover.

I am immensely proud of where I am now. I have grown immeasurably as a person and as a human being. I have learnt to deal with so many different things above and beyond my failed relationship. Maybe I've just grown up. I know that the road ahead will not always be trouble-free, but at least I am now better equipped to deal with the challenges in a much more confident and panic-free manner.

Setbacks

It's been a difficult period recently. After writing a self-congratulatory entry a few days ago, I fell into the trap of overthinking and becoming upset by events around me. Well, not so much events, but decisions that were being made that I had no control over. I felt trapped and powerless and it has taken me a couple of days to work through my issues. It seems that on this road to recovery from a major relationship event, there are lots of compromises to adjust to. Of course, it's always possible to walk away and spend the rest of your life looking for the perfect set of circumstances, but the problem is there is never the perfect set of circumstances and adaptation and compromise is all a part of life.

If we dig our heels in when the situation is obviously not in our favour, there could be a lot of resultant grief. It's all a matter of weighing up the pros and cons, but also trying to understand the other point of view. We might feel unjustly treated, but what we are demanding might be equally unjust. I guess it's all about levels of tolerance. If we feel really aggrieved and our wishes, completely ignored, it's difficult not to get upset and experience a sense of abandonment. This is particularly acute when we've offered to compromise, but those about us haven't. Why do we always end up being the person to compromise? There could be any number of reasons for this. Maybe we are better able to compromise because we're older and supposedly wiser. Maybe our compromise pails into insignificance compared to the compromises we are demanding. Yep, balance is the key.

It just goes to show that when you think you are doing well and the recovery process seems to be working, it doesn't take much to throw a spanner in the works. My cogs have certainly been chewed up in the last few days and I've lost my way yet again. Getting over a major betrayal is a rocky road of self-discovery and setbacks. Just when you think you are strong enough to cope, something crops up to undermine that confidence and send you in a tailspin of self-doubt and loneliness. Suddenly, those people you thought were there to support you don't support you and you feel isolated and without anywhere to turn.

I find life very lonely in these situations. I find myself particularly vulnerable after the biggest trauma in my life has left me trying to rebuild everything from scratch. The betrayal knocked me out and made me realise there isn't anyone in life you can trust but yourself. Everyone around us has their own set of priorities and many of them are not the same as ours. We need to be strong enough internally to cope. For some reason, other people seem to have support networks, but I don't. Self-reliance is the key. We come into this world alone and we leave it alone.

This diary is a warts and all account of heartbreak and it can't be anything else if it's going to be honest. Setbacks are a part of life and if we can't deal with them, it will be difficult to carry on. I've had some very positive times in this recovery process, but also some pretty negative ones. I'm hoping that my mood will lift and I will be back to writing interesting and uplifting entries in the future. The voyage of discovery continues…

Attachment

I had a busy period of work recently, culminating in saying goodbye to a number of people I've known for quite a few years. It was a sad occasion and there were a few moist eyes around. Saying goodbye is a difficult thing to do, particularly, if there are emotional attachments involved. But life moves on and circumstances change. Those people will live on in us and hopefully, we will have the opportunity to watch their progress at least from afar.

I've had a troubled few days emotionally, quite apart from saying fond goodbyes to people I care about. I've been tussling with old attachment issues. During the course of my marriage, I became totally attached to my wife. I loved her completely and unconditionally. In fact, I think I loved her as much as I loved my parents. I poured my heart and soul into the relationship and for 24 years, I felt secure in the knowledge that she would be part of my life forever. Even beyond forever, if that's possible. When my wife betrayed me, my attachment was left in tatters. And as I've pointed out before, losing someone you love from something other than death, turns your life upside down. There isn't any sense of conclusion or resolution. Your love has been rejected and abandoned and you feel helpless.

After such an experience, it's very difficult to fill that attachment gap. Letting go seems to take forever—if it can ever happen completely—and then what do you replace it with? In my case, it's probably another attachment because I'm longing for that sense of security all over again. But the set of circumstances that led to your first attachment is never going to be the same again and trying to replicate them is fruitless. Furthermore, the new person in your life isn't necessarily going to want you to try to recapture something that has gone. They don't want to be a replacement for your ex and quite rightly so. They are different people, with different emotional needs. Maybe because of their own life experiences, they actually want to avoid too much attachment. Not only that, perhaps deep down I'm scared of too much attachment—in case it is destroyed again—even though I seem to want it.

Pretty complicated stuff. What I do find valuable is talking about it with my partner. When we both understand why we react in certain ways when the emotional path gets a bit rocky, we are better able to deal with it. We both bring different things to our new relationship and we both bring different sorts of scars. Our reactions are triggered by those scars. With understanding comes the ability to deal with things openly and resolve any underlying issues. Often the external triggers have nothing to do with the root causes. We might be getting grumpy about something that has little to do with those deep-seated scars. The external trigger irritations disappear if we know what's caused them.

So many misunderstandings can be avoided if we only take the time to be open and honest with each other. We are who we are, and who we are is a result of our life experiences as much as our DNA. We react accordingly. Providing we are all on the same page, we can deal with attachment, non-attachment or any other issue with patience and understanding, and certainly not any form of conflict.

Whinging

Good morning, world! After a rather disrupted week, I'm ready to resume my quest to find some answers to life's conundrums. It just goes to show that no matter how confident I get, I still suffer from setbacks. I guess we all do and that's part of being alive. Everything in life is a matter of balance and it doesn't take much to put us off-kilter.

These wobbles can be a tiny, almost imperceptible deviation from our preordained path, or they can be a more major jolt that sends us in a completely different direction. One can be easily managed, the other takes a lot of time to adjust to. Every area of our lives can be affected, so the adjustment may need to happen across the board. Over the last couple of months, I've tried to chronicle some of the adjustments I've been trying to make after my long-term relationship ended. The fact that I'm still trying to deal with a situation that happened almost three years ago, is certainly a reflection of how major that jolt was.

I think by writing about these things in such a consistent manner for the last three months, I've tried to take the sting out of its tail. I've thought through so many things, I'm almost at a point where I'm sick of thinking about it. That's probably good for me and absolutely marvellous for anyone who is reading this diary! There comes a point where everyone gets sick of our whinging and it's time to really look forward and not back. I know it's been difficult and I know I have been through a lot, but hasn't everyone in some shape or form?

If I choose to continue with this diary, I might change its focus. I might not be able to change its title, but I think the content might need to morph into something a little more uplifting! Whinging can become very tiresome…sorry!

Problem Solving

Trying to stay optimistic in the face of setbacks can be a bit of a challenge. You never quite know when the next spanner in the works is going to arrive. One moment, we are sailing along without a worry in the world and the next, wham, bang and nothing seems easy. I think we've all spent our lives coping with these sorts of events. But as long as we know there isn't anything unusual about this, the better able we will be to cope.

I think I'm beginning to learn that the best way to deal with a problem is to face it full-on and solve it as quickly as possible. Don't ruminate for too long if it's something that can be resolved quickly. Delaying things tends to up stress levels, and stress and problems don't go very well together. However, even if it's a problem that needs some thought, the important thing to do is *make a decision* to delay the resolution. It's a bit like keeping your flights on hold whilst you sort out the finer details of your trip. It gives us pressure-less thinking time and avoids rash decisions.

I know so many people who avoid making a decision either way. They have all these unresolved issues niggling away at them and their stress levels must be extremely high. I often wonder how they cope and what such an arrangement achieves. Perhaps it's a way of solving multiple problems at once. Everything is just simmering away on a back burner and being processed unconsciously. Once the solutions are ready, it's all done in one fell swoop. Well, good luck to them, but it isn't the way I work.

I'm more of a deal-with-things-one-at-a-time guy. As each niggle is ticked off my list, my spirits begin to rise and I feel more confident to carry on. It's a cumulative thing that builds confidence. Admittedly, maybe the first problems might create some challenges, but even they can be overcome with a methodical approach. Dividing problems up into their elements and dealing with each one, step by step, stops the feeling of being overwhelmed and swamped by the enormity of it all. Every great journey begins with just one step and it's so true.

I think the people who have the confidence to make decisions quickly and easily are the ones who sail through life without too many hiccups. They have developed a model for problem-solving by initially going through the steps above. Logical and systematic steps that take the difficulty out of the problem. A problem is only a problem when it's unresolved. Resolve it quickly and effectively, and it disappears. After a while, the decisions required at each stage of problem-solving become quicker and quicker and they result in rapid resolution. The lucky ones develop an instinct for identifying the root cause of a problem and get to it fast.

If we take this approach, any problem is solvable, which means we aren't afraid to start, which means we'll be quicker to finish. I'm finished for today.

It's a No-Brainer

When I first started writing this diary, I did so with the intention of relieving the depression brought on by the failure of my marriage. I had struggled for many years trying to rid myself of the memories and heartache associated with this, the most painful period in my life. Even though I found a wonderful new partner, I was still being haunted on a daily basis by all the emotions associated with being betrayed. I just couldn't let go and move on successfully. At first, this diary expressed my anger and disbelief at the way my ex had behaved and how I just couldn't get to grips with the cruelty of it all. I developed techniques to block any thoughts of her so that I didn't spiral down into incredibly sad places. With these techniques, my moods lifted and I even managed almost two months of being relatively depression free. Blocking techniques do work but they require a lot of focus. They also require consistency, since no habit can be formed overnight—it takes a month or more to programme our neural highways into new patterns. Combined with the blocking techniques, writing my diary gave me an outlet for a lot of my pent-up emotions. Even though I was blocking those painful thoughts that stab you in the heart and make you feel physically ill, I could still think about things objectively and try to make some sense of the situation I found myself in.

Heartbreak Hotel has been a cathartic exercise and has helped me through some very difficult times. I have had various degrees of success and failure with the blocking techniques. Even though I knew they worked, I have often found myself drifting back into old habits and raking over the past. But despite these setbacks, the number of times I experience the gut-wrenching flushes of regret, grief and longing are diminishing, as are the times of waking up in the morning with a knot in my stomach. But often, there is still an overall feeling of emptiness and loss even though years have passed and I wonder if these feelings will ever go away. I keep reminding myself that life without my ex is what I make of it, life isn't dependent on my ex. I also try to remind myself that whatever happened was out of my control and she made no effort to save what we had. In her mind, our marriage was doomed—even after 24 years together—and that was that. But it is a very black-and-white mindset that I just can't seem to comprehend.

I know it's my problem and unless I move on, the rest of my life will be one of emptiness and regret. My wonderful, kind and loyal new partner will be playing second fiddle to my memories and that's appalling. If I continue to speculate about what could have been, instead of embracing what is, I really will slowly die of a broken heart. However, maybe I'm being too hard on myself. Maybe I'm not the only kind-hearted and sensitive soul who is still struggling to recover after quite a few years. Maybe the glacial rate this recovery process takes is just the way it is for some people? Maybe because it's taking me so long to get over my heartbreak, it's an indication of how 'in love' I was and that's nothing to be ashamed of.

Lots of questions and no definitive answers. The expression 'it is what it is' can be very helpful in these situations. Sometimes, there are no answers and the only thing that helps us through these difficult times, is time itself. I have expended literally thousands of hours thinking about my past rather than thinking about my here and now and indeed, my future. I have the ability to enhance my now and my future, but not my past. It seems pretty pointless to spend time in a place that can never exist anymore, along with someone who can never exist anymore. Much better to be fully committed to someone who does exist and cares about me, rather than think about someone who dumped me and who ceased to care about me a long time ago. It's a no brainer really.

Taking Stock

Yesterday, I started an entry but didn't manage to finish it. I've struggled to find the words recently and to find the motivation to continue. I guess that after 80-odd diary entries, I'm beginning to wonder if I still have something valuable to say. When self-doubt sets in, it's difficult to continue doing anything. But having read through some of my past entries, including the more recent ones, they aren't half as bad as I imagined they were. Life is like that; it generally isn't half as bad as we think it is. Maybe it's because we are so close to what's going on, or maybe it's because we're actually part of what's going on? Stepping back and looking at things objectively once the dust has settled is a very good thing to do.

It's just so easy to give up. Life is full of challenges and when you face one after another, they tend to wear you down. They chip away at your resolve and your ability to cope. Whilst it's all happening, you carry on carrying on without much idea of how well you are managing. It's only once the succession of challenges is over that you can really appreciate how much you've achieved, and this is a very important thing to do. Taking stock of these mini-triumphs is paramount since it gives you the confidence to carry on. It's also important that we are not too hard on ourselves. When our spirits are low, our motivation dwindles and with it the ability to achieve anything. Even the things that aren't half as bad as we think they are, tend to be seen as useless. By taking stock, we are seeing the bigger picture, and with it, gaining an understanding of our strengths more than our weaknesses.

So many of the important things in life happen at a glacial rate and in a fast-moving world, this can be incredibly frustrating. We've become accustomed to fast everything: fast food, fast internet, fast cars and fast resolution to life's problems. But some things take time and we need to realise that we're still making progress, even if the progress is incremental. Taking stock of those incremental steps is what lets us off the hook. Looking back on my previous diary entries helps to give me the confidence to carry on. Besides, writing is like everything in life, the more you do it, the better you get. The more challenges we face and resolve, the more adept we will become at coping. Keep going and keep taking stock.

Saying Goodbye to the Fairy Tale

I dreamt about my ex again last night. It's becoming a little bit disconcerting as this is the third night in a row that she has occupied my subconscious mind, although, with the subconscious mind, it's difficult to know how much brain space she continues to take up. Whatever it is, it's far too much. After almost three years, this woman has no right to be haunting me in such a cruel way. Why can't she just leave me alone to get on with the rest of my life? Why on earth would I give her the time of day, let alone the time of night? What spell has this witch cast over me?

I think the answers to these questions are very complicated but probably worth exploring nonetheless. Of course, one thing is for sure, first love is difficult to get over, particularly one that lasted 24 years. I was a late starter in the love department and I didn't fall madly and deeply in love until I was in my 30s. I'd always been waiting for that perfect person to spend the rest of my life with and I thought I'd hit the jackpot with my ex. With little experience of love, I threw myself into the relationship with everything I had. There was no holding back or caution, just total commitment. That head-over-heels devotion stayed in place for the whole of the time we were together; there was absolutely nothing in my mind that could break it. I certainly didn't think she would break it. I guess that's part of the problem and why these flashbacks keep occurring. When you yourself are so committed and loyal, you never expect your other half to be anything other than that too, particularly, as you'd shared so many amazing times together and the world thought you were inseparable. I actually thought we were inseparable. My ex, however, had different ideas.

First love then, is one of the elements that keep things lingering on in someone like me. It's pretty powerful stuff and very difficult to shake off. I think hopeless romantics are a dying breed, but I'm happy to become extinct if I stay true to myself. I guess the problem arises when the magic goes out of the relationship for the one we love. One or more triggers switch off the love bug for them and we are left high and dry. After our divorce, I always thought that given time, the love bug would wither away and die, even for me. But maybe it's just taking a bit more time than I imagined. When someone has betrayed you and hurt you so, so much, you'd think it would be pretty easy to forget about them.

That's one of life's conundrums, and no doubt, one I will continue to grapple with for a very long time. I sometimes think I'm perpetuating things deliberately because I'm still in love with the idea of eternal love. I'm still in love with the idea of first and one and only love. Of course, this is quite unsettling because I feel I'm being disloyal to my new partner, who is a wonderful, kind, caring and very understanding woman. My love for her is what matters, not my love for an ideal that has ceased to exist—I said these things were complicated! I think part of the letting go process involves letting go of our original dream, as much as the person themselves. My dreams are therefore expressions of my longing for my original ideal, not a longing for my ex. With that in mind, I feel a lot better.

There are those of us who tend to idealise the past at the expense of living in the present and looking forward to the future. We too easily forget the pain and the heartbreak of betrayal and try to hang onto an ideal that doesn't exist. Life is not a fairy tale of one and only love that lasts forever. It's not a fairy tale of unshakable loyalty and utter devotion. It's a grittier affair, full of disappointment and challenges. It's full of people who change and leave us behind in the process. But nonetheless, it's also full of amazing opportunities and amazing people. It's up to us to learn to adapt and accept things that are beyond our control. It's up to us to embrace the new love in our life and be thankful for a wonderful second chance.

Being Patient

It's very easy to give up on life after a severe bout of heartbreak. I know I'm making it sound a bit like the flu, which is nasty, but something we will eventually get over. However, if you are like me, with heartbreak, there are times when you think it's just going to linger on forever. I also feel guilty saying such things as it smacks of self-indulgence and weakness; feelings that should have long gone three years after my 24-year marriage ended. Perhaps, I'm just weak and self-indulgent and I really do want to spend the rest of my life feeling sorry for myself. Somehow, I don't think that's the case. I've tried every trick in the book to get over my ex, from blocking techniques (never thinking about her) to writing a daily diary about my experiences. Nonetheless, here I am once again facing the same issues.

I don't want to spend the rest of my life in some kind of duality, one half of me living with my wonderful new partner and the other half still trapped in the past with memories of my ex. It's not fair to my partner and it's not fair to me. Why have some people got this amazing ability to move on, while others, like me—and possibly you—have to suffer endless torture of regret and grief? It really isn't fair. I dreamt about my ex again last night and this is where the conscious blocking techniques don't work. It was the usual sort of dream trying to find her in a crowd and not succeeding. It's probably got a heap of psychological abandonment issues associated with it. But what am I to do? Go and see another counsellor and have them tell me there is nothing wrong with me that time won't heal, or else I've just got to live with it? That doesn't seem very satisfactory.

I think there is a certain amount of self-destruction involved, because it makes us victims, which, to a certain extent we are. I think we want our ex to feel guilty for potentially ruining our lives. We want them to take responsibility for their actions and admit that they were wrong. We secretly want them to be feeling as bad about the whole situation as we do. Unfortunately, such delusion just perpetuates our plight. Why should it matter to us what they're thinking or feeling anyway—if they do in fact have any feelings? It matters because we rather perversely want them still to have some regard for us. After all, we shared all that time together and much of it was happy. The trouble is, we are not grasping the essence of their mindset, which has an enormous capacity to switch off and cover things up with self-delusion. They needed to convince themselves it was our fault in order to betray us. They needed to convince themselves that they did all they could to save our marriage, even when they didn't. They have convinced themselves that 'it was all for the best.' Excuse me, but that's a load of twaddle.

However, twaddle or not, they are living their lives happily (presumably) and we have all this baggage still tormenting us. I know, I just need to pull myself together and forget about the whole sordid experience. Man up and carry on. If only life were so simple. I guess by sharing my experiences, I'm trying to come to terms with them. I'm hoping I'm not the only emotional wreck out there, trying to get their life back on track. I certainly feel better after writing my diary entries and even reviewing the large number I've already written. I might not be any closer to a solution to my broken heart, but at least having discussed the issues, I'm aware of how much I have actually grown as a person. For the first two and a half years, I was a blubbering mess and it took very little to set me off. The waterworks have ceased to gush so readily and the stabs of pain are less intense. It's all there below the surface, but at least, it's under control.

Maybe the moral of today's story is that time is a great healer, but we need to be very patient. For sensitive souls like us, very, very patient. Hopefully, the good people that are now around us will continue to understand what an incredible amount of adjustment all of this takes. I just hope that this toughening-up exercise doesn't make me into a cold heartless person like my ex—now that would be really sad. But somehow, I don't think that's going to happen and if it takes me a bit longer to cope and still retain my sensibilities, I'm happy to be patient.

Tally-Ho!

I had a good sleep last night but it was quite a busy night with dreams. Nothing sinister, but nothing really memorable either. I often wonder what dreams achieve and whether we'd all be better off without them. But they are what they are and represent yet another thing we need to accept, as we can't do much about them. There will always be certain things in our life that are beyond our control. We either accept them or let them drive us crazy.

I think when a major trauma happens in life, there needs to be a certain amount of acceptance. The end of a relationship is something that can either finish us off or change the direction we take in life. I'm still struggling getting over my 24-year relationship after three years of heartache. I still wake up in the morning wondering what's the point carrying on. I'd invested so much in my ex and our life together that starting from scratch again is still proving to be a struggle. I am getting there slowly, but it is ever-so-slowly. It's the whole 'letting go' thing, I guess, and letting go is difficult if you held on so firmly for so long. I went for a two-hour walk yesterday and it did me a universe of good. It made me realise that the world is a wonderful place and that we can learn a lot from nature and the simple things in life. We can make our own world so complicated if we want to. We can create complications that don't need to exist and traumatise ourselves with memories of the past and worries about the present and the future. The birds and dogs on the beach made me realise that they were happy in the here and now. I doubt the seagull fishing just behind the breakers was thinking about yesterday's breakfast and I doubt that the dogs fetching sticks were comparing their efforts with the day before. They were just happy enjoying the moment. If only we could be the same. It's a real privilege to be alive and one that we shouldn't destroy with unnecessary rubbish that can spoil our enjoyment of it. Every moment is precious and every moment should be savoured. The people in our lives right now are the important ones, not the ones in our past, be they alive or dead. Of course, we can look back with affection on those who have gone and who made us the people we are today, they will be with us forever in a nice way. But as for wasting our time lamenting the loss of people who actually hurt and betrayed us, that's plain stupid and a waste of our precious present and a possible destruction of our wonderful future.

I'm convinced that the people that really have life sussed are those who can move forward and not look back. It's the people who grab life with both hands and run with it no matter what setbacks they face. The birds on the beach don't sit around ruminating about the fish they lost three years ago and the dogs don't sit around berating themselves for not swimming out far enough to get that special stick three years ago. Stupid or what? Like a dog's daily exercise, we must constantly remind ourselves of these self-evident truths. Life goes on and we can choose to go on with it or wither up and die. We can hop on the train and enjoy the ride, or sit at home moping. It's our choice. Life will go on with or without us and it's our choice.

Part of the reason for writing these diary entries is to keep reminding myself of these fundamental things. I need to keep hammering it home that the only one losing out on life is me if I don't board the train of life and enjoy the journey. Why should the people who hurt us have a fantastic life at our expense? Why should they carry on regardless and leave us hurting about everything? Well, the answer is it doesn't matter what they do or don't do, it matters what we do or don't do. We are masters of our own fate and if we choose to fly like a bird and have fun like a dog, we can. The rotten people who hurt us only have control over us if we let them. They have done their worst and we are still alive. Let them rot in their own wrongdoing for the rest of their lives and meanwhile let's jump aboard life's great adventure and lavish our energies on the people who matter to us now. The people who love us and won't betray us. The people who are worth living for, because we are well rid of the ones who betrayed us. Tally-Ho!

Expunging the Pointless

I'm sorry, but I'm feeling a bit down this morning and I'm hoping that by writing this diary entry, I might be able to lift my spirits a bit. I think it's often difficult to put a finger on exactly what causes these mood swings as it's such a gradual process. It might be a word here or a word there that wears away at our optimism. The people speaking the words might not even be aware of what they're doing, but slowly but surely the words mount up and obviously eat away at our core. To be sure, we probably need to have a certain propensity to listen to these words and thus allow them to change our mood.

I had a long walk yesterday and although I felt tired towards the end of it, I still felt exhilarated. My walks are never thought-free of course, and frequently involve rehashing the past. If the beach is empty of people, I might even indulge in the odd rant, berating out loud my ex for screwing up my life so adroitly. Needless to say, I sometimes feel a bit guilty indulging in such behaviour as it does have tinges of madness about it. I'll always do a quick check front back and sides to make sure I've not been spotted by some other clandestine walker taking a rest in the dunes. As I've witnessed other people talking to themselves first-hand, it's not really a confidence-building sight. In fact, I tend to steer clear of such types with a vengeance. But when the coast is clear, it's an amazing feeling to be able to let rip and express just how disappointed we are in our ex as a human being. You can bottle things up only so much before it's time for a good verbal exorcism. For me, after almost three years in the fall-out zone, it's not all venomous hatred, there is now a funny kind of forgiveness involved. I say funny kind, because I don't think there will ever be full-blown forgiveness, but maybe that will change with time, I hope so.

Was this part of my slip back into the dark zone? I don't think so. I think that was more to do with the meal I had with friends in the evening. These are friends I shared with my ex for many years, so they know us both pretty well. To be honest, I don't have many of these mutual friends left. Partly because I don't want to hear about my ex through them and partly because I just don't want to be reminded of anything associated with her. Often in their desire to be fair to both parties, they feel compelled to give me her side of the story in innuendo-laden remarks that cut to the bone. I usually manage to keep my composure, but the pain is there regardless and each innuendo-ridden comment nibbles away at my self-esteem. Avoidance of these people has been the only course of action and whilst it's sad to lose friends you have known for a long time, it's sometimes necessary for one's mental health.

However, it isn't always the innuendo that takes its toll. It's also the negative thinking and mental ruts that many of these people share. There is a bleakness about the conversation that isn't particularly uplifting. The same old rivalries emerge and the same old power struggles along with them. It takes me back to those 'keeping up with the Joneses' times, where everything is a competition to be the top dog. It's a fake way of living that isn't part of my world anymore. I'm not interested in taking up the bait. I don't want to compete with anyone. I don't want to be put in a position of needing to defend myself or my abilities. I am who I am, warts and all. Like me for that, or don't like me at all. Likewise, I'm not interested in demeaning other people in order to feel some weird sort of self-importance. What's the point?

So, there you have it. I woke up this morning having slept on a pile of negative influences that had gnawed away at my optimism levels overnight. Each little remark had chipped away at my resolve to be happy and productive. Having identified these triggers, I feel a lot better. So, you see, it's never a matter of just random depression, there's always a reason. If we can identify the reasons, we have a good chance of looking at them objectively and seeing them for what they are: nonsense and something to expunge from our day as quickly as possible.

Keep Things Simple

It's once again an early start for me, hoping to come up with a theme for today's ruminations. I never quite know how things will go, and recently, I've had a few days off simply because I started something and couldn't finish it. Maybe the drafts will be of use in the future, but who knows? I don't know much about anything these days. When you think you've got life sorted, something comes along and makes it all a mess. It's a messy business living. But the alternatives aren't worth considering, at least from my point of view.

We're an amazing mix of chemicals and when one or two of them are out of balance, it's enough to send us off into a chemical-induced tailspin. I've never taken any drugs for depression, so have no idea what they're like. I'm really cautious about mucking about with nature, although I've never been averse to alcohol, or the odd Panadol to soothe some of the consequences of overindulging in that particular drug. To be honest, I have a bit of a headache this morning from having four glasses of wine last night. I'm not sure the wine was that good, so that might be part of the problem.

I think this idea that we are all just lumps of meat driven by a complicated mix of chemicals is an interesting one. I wonder what controls these chemicals and why more of one sort are manufactured in our bodies above another. Why do some people manufacture a heap of endorphins naturally, and others don't? I guess there are certain lifestyle choices we make that help. Exercise encourages the manufacture of endorphins and they can have the same effect as morphine. Maybe if I go for a walk right now, my headache will go? Rather than using Paracetamol as an analgesic, I should go for a bike ride. Interesting concepts, but sometimes a little impractical. But joking aside, if we look at the bigger picture of who we are and the way we function, maybe we'll be better able to cope with a life that gets complicated and messy.

Everything is about perspective. Everything is about the information we receive and process through our five senses—and the sixth when it kicks in every now and then. A lot of what we do on a daily basis is automated. We function without really knowing about it and that's kind of nice. I'm very grateful to my body for taking the responsibility away from my thinking mind when it comes to bodily functions. It all just happens and then I can get on with more important things like writing my diary.

We need to count our blessings in so many ways living how most of us do now. Regardless of automated bodily functions, our ancestors probably didn't have the time to have airy-fairy thoughts about the meaning of life. They were too busy trying to stay alive. Maybe that's it? Maybe our species has become so sophisticated that we have too much time on our hands? The need to fight to stay alive has gone. The need to forage for our next meal has gone. The trouble is, although life has got easier in the physical sense, it's got a hell of a lot more complicated in the mental sense. Our minds are no longer solely focused on keeping us alive, they are free to overthink and make things that are not complicated, complicated. And with all these complicated thoughts, we start to upset the natural balance in our mind and body that used to exist. We've become a society of short-circuited people and I'm probably a prime example.

Maybe that's just it? Maybe if I put myself back in Primordial times and with primeval thinking, I'd never have spent the last three years processing the end of my 24-year relationship? I probably wouldn't have thought about it for more than three days. In fact, I'd most likely have just grabbed my biggest club, found my wife's lover and given him a good going over and that would have been the end of the matter. Instant justice in an instant age—an age where there was no time for touchy-feely heartbreak therapy. To be honest, I've never been tempted by that approach because thank heavens, we're not living in such brutal times anymore. Besides, that sort of justice never targets all the criminals in that scenario. But, as an overarching thought, it does make one wonder how much our modern-day overthinking adds to our pain, rather than alleviating it.

Keeping things simple is therefore the answer in any situation. Whilst grabbing our favourite club for rapid retribution is no longer an option, we can certainly take heed of the sentiments behind this approach. Our best and only revenge, is a quick and painless psychological resolution to life's challenges. We need to realise that the longer we let the hurt and pain remain, the less of life we'll retain. Our ancestors were fighting for their lives and so are we, just in a different way.

Inner Strength

I woke up with feelings of unease this morning and I really wish I could stop this from happening. It's as if my world isn't settled and I'm afraid of something. Unfortunately, I've been weak recently and I've indulged in thoughts of the past and that has probably prompted these abandonment episodes. Will I ever learn? I must look ahead and not back; I must practice what I preach; I must block and bury the past or I'll end up living in a constant state of unease.

As a home-loving Cancerian, I've always cherished stability, I think we all do in one form or another. When a major emotional trauma hits us, our whole life gets turned upside down. The person you trusted implicitly betrays you and you then feel as if there is nothing permanent in life. Those amazing feelings of safety and comfort suddenly disappear and the world becomes a bleak and very lonely place to inhabit. Perhaps it just takes time to re-establish another safe environment and mend the old wounds of abandonment. I certainly shouldn't be feeling any unease because I've been incredibly lucky and have found a new partner who is kind, loving and caring. She is also loyal and incredibly understanding of my still fragile emotional state.

I think it takes a long time to build a nest and feel secure in it. When my former wife ended our marriage, I left with practically no material possessions as I couldn't face seeing things that reminded me of my previous life. Whilst it was a fresh start, I'm sure there are scars that need to heal. There are also mindsets that need to change. Material possessions are not what matter in life and there is no inherent strength in them. Strength comes from within, not from without. Strength also comes from stable relationships, not from comfortable home environments. I think that's probably where I've been going wrong. When thoughts of the past haunt me, I tend to remember the feelings of stability rather than the increasingly rocky times. I yearn for the kind of stability that was built up over a period of decades. However, it's a stability memory that really has no substance, but lingers on regardless.

Inner strength is the nub of the matter. There are countless stories of people who have endured incredible depravity—physically and mentally—but have survived pretty much because of their inner strength. They created their security from within and it didn't matter what was going on around them. We all need to be like that and I need to find ways of restoring this kind of inner strength. I think it starts with deciding what values really matter in life and having the vision and determination to uphold them. Material things are irrelevant to people with inner strength because they know that such things come and go so easily. In fact, everything in life that is external to us can easily come and go. So many external things in our lives are completely out of our control. No matter how we try, we can't alter the outcome. But if we have core strength, it really doesn't matter how things turn out because we'll always be able to deal with any eventuality.

I think my panic attacks are a result of compromised inner strength. I am still hankering after some distant stability cocoon that kept me feeling safe, but was in fact an illusion. I relied on my ex rather than myself. To be fair, I thought it was a reciprocal agreement and I provided as much stability for her as she did for me. But come crunch time, she sought stability elsewhere. I guess my panic attacks also indicate that I'm a bit scared of my ability to cope. What I thought would never happen, happened, and I'm terrified it might happen again. Of course, there is no earthly reason for this because I'm in a totally different relationship with a totally different woman. My wonderful new partner understands heartbreak herself and recognises the recovery process. She is giving me the space to find myself again or maybe even find myself for the first time.

Self-discovery is an amazing journey and one that requires space. It isn't something anyone else can help you with. Maybe the uneasy feelings will subside when I have restored my inner strength or at the very least started the process. There are so many external things to grapple with in life, but all the answers ultimately come from within.

Let's Start

Good morning, world! Today, I'm going to go completely heartbreak free. I've had enough of writing about such a depressing subject and repeating all the same things over and over and over and over again. It's time to live life, not dwell in the past. Life is what we make of it, and we should make a lot of it. Grab every opportunity and run with it. Have fun in the process and enjoy the amazing people we meet on the way. Every day is a new start in life and it doesn't matter what happened yesterday, we have the possibility of anything if we have the right mindset. The sun is out and optimism rules.

I am finally realising that any change can be made in an instant if we only make the effort. There is nothing physically different about me today compared to yesterday. I still have two legs, two arms a body and a head—a few other things besides of course. However, the person yesterday was moping about thinking about the past and the person today isn't going to do that. It's my choice and it's your choice to feel in whatever way you like. Much better to be bright and optimistic than dull and depressed. These states don't need to depend on any other stimulant than ourselves. We have it within us to snap out of bad mental sets and enjoy life. It's so easy to spend our time stewing over things that can't be changed rather than focusing on things that can make our lives fantastic. Why bother with the former when the latter is there for the taking?

I talked about inner strength recently and that's what it all boils down to. Taking command of our lives rather than letting other people choose the direction we take. Very often, it is those who have left us that are still controlling us. It's time to discard their wicked influence and carve out our future with confidence and certainty. There is no earthly reason why we shouldn't live a very happy and fulfilled life free of the past and free of those toxic influences from the past. The future is toxic-free and a blank canvas for us to create wonderful things. The only place to start is here. The only time to start is now. So, let's start!

Dumping Introspection

I had a good walk on the beach yesterday and felt energised during and afterwards. It's amazing how exhilarating this can be, with the wind blowing through your hair and nothing but the birds for company. It creates a freedom that's hard to beat. I intend to do the same thing today.

I'm not even going to bother telling you what I dreamt about last night as it has no relevance to how I'm going to spend my day. My subconscious mind might be still dwelling on the past, but I'm determined my conscious mind won't. Heartbreak leaves so many memory scars that are easily re-ignited. Just one thought is enough to send shivers through your whole body and if we are silly enough to follow on, one thought can lead to multiple thoughts that all have the same effect. I find myself slipping into this bad habit early in the morning and if I persist, it can change my mood for the day. The only way is forward and the only way we can lead a happy and productive life is by leaving those memories behind us.

I am convinced that we can't actually deal with our relatively recent heartbreak memories. I've tried this approach and it just doesn't work. I thought that I could take individual memories and deal with them, one by one. But it simply isn't possible to cope with such things at this point in time. One thought leads to another and we once again end up in a dark place. Forget about your painful past and concentrate on your happy future. Live one day at a time and find different things to celebrate every day. I know this sounds all very touchy-feely, but it really is the only way. I've tried every way I can to understand what happened to me and I'm still none the wiser. I've tried to comprehend the processes that led to my darkest hours and I can't. I've apportioned blame, I've taken responsibility and I'm still struggling.

I have realised that I am only happy when I am not thinking about the past. This is so obvious, but often so difficult to manage. We have an inbuilt inclination (well, I do anyway) to analyse what happened, and all it creates is pain. It's as if we enjoy the pain and how silly is that? We end up in a constant state of pain and cease to enjoy our life right now. This constant state of pain also reduces our desire to grab whatever opportunities come our way. We end up missing the here and now and missing the good times that could be there for us if we just put the processes in place. We also fail to recognise what are our strengths because our self-esteem has sunk to such a low level. Heartbreak has left us empty and weak and it keeps us this way if we continue to revisit the battleground.

We all have talents that we can share with other people and that's the most important way forward. After all, what else are we here for? Satisfying lives come from helping to make the world a better place for those around us. It doesn't come from being selfish. It's amazing how much better we feel after helping someone else, be it a family member, friend or even a complete stranger. Our energy levels increase and I'm sure our endorphins with it. Introspection is selfish and it actually doesn't do us any good, so I for one will try my best to avoid it. Let's all find a purpose in life that helps other people and then we'll all be happy.

Substituting Bad with Good

Yesterday, I had a great two-hour walk along the beach and I hit upon some very interesting ideas. It was a great day: the sky was clear and the sun warm, with a gentle breeze keeping things cool but comfortable. I started with clear intentions of ignoring any thoughts about my past and certainly any that contained my ex. Then suddenly, I realised that if I replaced my ex with my lovely new partner in my memories, I can actually start to enjoy them. It's such a simple concept, but a miraculous one! All those stresses and strains that my ex used to create wouldn't exist with my wonderful new partner. Everything would be so easy-going and harmonious. I then started to wonder if it was actually my ex I was missing, or the places we went to.

If it isn't my ex and it's just the places, what on earth am I getting upset about? That's precisely it. We mustn't hanker after things we've already done; we should look forward to the things we are going to do. And if we choose to revisit some of the places that made a big impression on us, like Paris or Venice or the Amalfi Coast, then we can look forward to enjoying them so much more without the bullying, nagging, guilt trips and temper tantrums. We can enjoy them with an immensely talented, kind, caring and loving person, rather than a lying, cheating and incredibly manipulative person. What an amazing future to look forward to.

I think there are so many things that contribute to the heartbreak we feel after a long-term relationship has ended. If we are betrayed, there are natural feelings of self-deprecation and loathing. We blame ourselves for things that weren't our fault. Instead, we must be strong and remember the betrayal and the hurt and the appalling way that we were treated. We must remember the lies and the manipulation, the coldness and cruelty. We need to substitute the overarching love we felt for our ex with distaste. We need to despise them for doing what they did to us and realise that our heartbreak that lingers on is unwarranted. We might be thinking of them hundreds of times a day and they probably don't give

218

us a second thought. They are heartless and cruel individuals that don't deserve anything from us anymore.

Let's replace them in all our memories with our new love, who absolutely deserves to be there. Furthermore, let's make bigger and better memories with our new love and look forward to an amazing life ahead, devoid of stress, tension, humiliation and crooked thinking. We deserve this and our new love deserves this too. They are loving and supporting us now. They are not wretched people like our ex, they are what real relationships are all about.

Doing Time

When you spend almost two and a half decades with someone in a really close relationship, it's very hard to let go. There are so many shared memories and emotions of both happiness and pain. The other person becomes a part of you because they have been a significant part of your life. Everything in the world reminds you of them because you shared everything for such a long period of time. Our task as the jilted party is to try to rebuild our lives in a meaningful way and understand that just because something is over, life doesn't cease to be filled with amazing possibilities.

It's an obvious opening statement in an ongoing discourse about betrayal and failed relationships. But sometimes, the obvious is the easiest thing to miss. Our heartbreak at losing someone who was so important to us completely clouds the issues and leaves us in a state of limbo, hardly able to function effectively. It seems that everything we do is tinged with sadness and when we try to make plans for the future, they seem empty and devoid of meaning. Our world has been frozen in a time capsule and our lives put on hold. It's really a tragic outcome to a tragic turn of events. It's also an indictment of those who allowed it to happen. They either didn't know us well enough to realise the impact their actions would have, or they didn't care. And that's a really bad reflection on their character.

Whichever way you look at it, the problem is theirs. I often wonder how they manage to cope with the scope of their betrayal and how they live with themselves. It takes a certain kind of coldness to expunge over two decades of closeness. It takes an amazing coldness to hurt a person who was obviously devoted to you. For me, it's one of life's mysteries and one that I will probably never comprehend. I realise that in the course of these diary entries, I've been trying to comprehend a lot of things and that's probably part of the problem. I'm trying to make sense of the situation from my point of view because I can't make sense of it from theirs. They have either made peace with themselves or are consumed with guilt. I'm not quite sure which I'd prefer it to be.

But whatever it is, that's their concern and not mine. I have spent more than enough time in limbo land. I have spent more than enough time feeling sad, empty and my life devoid of meaning. I have actually spent more than enough time blaming myself for something I didn't instigate, and taking responsibility for their heartless actions. Enough is enough. If I was in any way responsible for what transpired, I've done my time and I've paid the price. I can at least consider myself a reformed character. I wonder if she will ever be able to say the same thing.

Regardless of her feelings (if she has any), life must go on and maybe limbo land has been a necessary experience in order to recover. It's been a time to rebuild our emotional networks after the trauma and concentrate on what matters in life. We have missed the obvious because of the confusion that ensued. However, the mist is lifting and with it the realisation that sometimes we will never be able to understand another person's actions. Once we understand that, we'll understand how to move forward.

Shipwrecked

I wonder what it would be like to be the only person shipwrecked on a desert island. We would only have our thoughts for company and endless amounts of time to contemplate what we'd left behind. The strong amongst us would learn to forage for ourselves, initially finding food and then materials to build a shelter. Contemplation would be a luxury after the bare necessities of life were met. Weaker people would spend their time blaming fate for their situation and convincing themselves that the outside world would rescue them. Who would ultimately survive?

Life is a bit like this and we often find ourselves in situations that are completely beyond our control. Whether we have been physically shipwrecked or emotionally shipwrecked, or indeed both, we must be strong enough to forage our way out of either situation. I really don't think the sitting around and waiting to be rescued option is tenable. There have been countless books written, and movies made, about this very thing. The people that survive are the ones who have the strength of character to survive, and it really is strength of character more than physical prowess. When push comes to shove, it's a steely mental determination that pulls people through, not their physical attributes. The reason for our success as a species lies in our capacity to use our brains to solve problems. Our Neanderthal predecessors were physically more robust but lacked the ability to talk or use symbolic thought.

Our brain is therefore our greatest asset, even in a physically challenging situation. Every imaginable human triumph has been the result of thinking through the problem and coming up with a solution. The pyramids were built this way: An almost impossible feat of engineering was accomplished without modern machinery even in the distant past. Today, we fly around the world in sophisticated tin cans and build incredibly complex buildings because of thought. Designing the buildings and designing the tools to build the buildings. The human brain is miraculous. Ultimately, if we can use our minds correctly, we can achieve anything.

Back on our physical desert island, we can either harness our thoughts constructively and plan for the future, or we can wait around to be rescued and probably waste away and die. I know which option I want to choose.

The Coalface of Life

I'm really grateful to all the people that have supported me over the years. It isn't possible to achieve anything in life without people who believe in us. They are often the unsung heroes in our story. Some support us anonymously, while others like parents, brothers, sisters, partners and friends more openly. But in whatever category, they are all so important in making us the people we are today. Getting through life can be a challenge from within and from without. We are constantly up against our internal demons of self-doubt and what seem to be endless external forces that seem determined to hold us back.

I've been a self-help book junkie for years, in fact, for as long as I can remember. I was always searching for some magic cocktail of words that would energise my existence and allow me to become a meaningful and productive member of society. This probably came about from being a very shy, home-schooled child. I wasn't good with people and probably enjoyed my own company more than others. Growing up with a dog helped of course, as he became my constant companion. I didn't need to relate to other people or consciously foster friendships, my dog was enough. Going off to college in a big city many hours away from home was difficult and very scary. I was a country bumpkin and city life was alien to me. But what was more alien, was living in a hostel full of other eighteen-year-old strangers. Fortunately, I had a room of my own and could escape the dangers that lurked out in the corridor. I could listen at the door for any signs of life and make a dash for the bathroom or kitchen when the coast was clear. My first year was one of avoidance and trying to keep as low a profile as possible. However, inevitably, the more socialised around me tried to entice me out of my shell and over time, things got easier. By my second year, I was sharing a flat with four other students and at least dipping my toe into student life. Alcohol was my friend—it was for most of us—and that helped oil the wheels of social interaction and gave me the courage I seemed to lack.

I'm extremely grateful to the small group of friends I made during those early days away from home. They had all enjoyed 'normal' highly social upbringings and probably knew all about loners like me. Their constant encouragement and support were important to me at a difficult time of transition. At that stage, I was never destined to be the life and soul of a party, but for the most part, I managed to hold my own and even constantly strive to do as well as I could with my studies. I think my teachers did their best too, but may have been a bit exasperated by my dreamy approach to everything. I discovered that you could be just as anonymous in a big city as you could be in a deserted woodland. The city became my new wilderness to be explored on a daily basis. Hours and hours of walking and hours and hours of observing how people went about their daily lives. It was totally fascinating and much more interesting than what I was studying. In hindsight, I was gaining another degree in Anthropology without knowing it. But as I've said, I still realised how lucky I was to be doing what I was and pushed myself accordingly. Despite my surface lack of confidence and relatively poor social skills, a red-hot furnace of ambition burned within.

So, even in those early years, I always appreciated the encouragement and support I received. My parents were wonderful of course, but they gave way to other influences in my life and that has never changed. I have always tried to stay loyal to the important people in my life and to remain in touch with the oldest of friends and teachers. It's not always possible of course, but part of them remains a part of me nonetheless.

Being a self-help book junkie must have helped towards liberating me from shyness. I don't have any problem with social situations anymore and I don't even need alcohol for Dutch Courage. The biggest growth factor has occurred through being brave enough to challenge myself and having the courage to fail. All the theoretical advice in the world won't be a patch on practical experience. We ultimately learn at the coalface of life, not up in the office shuffling papers. Every aspect of our learning process is basically trial and error. If we don't try, we'll never know if something works or not. The recovery process from heartbreak is no exception. Every day is a challenge to find some new way of dealing with our anguish and every day we get closer to a solution, even if it doesn't seem that way at the time.

Acceptance (3)

It's been pouring down here for days on end and this kind of weather doesn't really encourage a bright spirit. Having said that, there is a certain charm about sitting inside all snuggled up, tapping away at the computer whilst the rain oscillates between light and heavy showers. There's a funny feeling of comfort and security and providing we don't need to venture out, there's also a feeling of contentment. There isn't much we can do about it, so acceptance is the only sensible course of non-action.

In many ways, this is a natural corollary for life itself. Getting frustrated by the rain is pointless and getting frustrated with what life throws up for us is equally pointless. If we give into every little niggle, we're in for a rough ride. For a very long time, I've been a firm believer in taking the sting out of tensions tail. Stress is a killer and if we don't find ways to defuse it, we're in for more than a rough ride, we're in for a swift end. Frustration is of course just one of the hallmarks of stress. Resentment is another. Why am I stuck inside when I could be out walking the beach? Why has it decided to rain for days when I'd planned to go camping? Why does the world around me always do the opposite of what I want it to? Why wasn't I born rich? Why didn't my parents give me a better education? Why am I so ugly, fat, or skinny? Why don't people appreciate what I do for them? The catalogue of grievances is endless. Ultimately, the only question we should really be asking ourselves is: why should I care?

Acceptance is the key to diffusing any form of tension and stress. Acceptance is a matter of coming to terms with what's offered, but most importantly, then making the most of what's offered. So, it's raining outside, which means I can do all the jobs around the house I've been meaning to do for ages. So, it's going to be raining for the next few days and the campsite is booked. It might be fun camping in the rain and waking up to that wonderful smell of petrichor when it eventually stops, or I can cancel the trip and stay at home snuggled up by the fire with my favourite book.

Once again, it's all about our mindset and not about what's happening around us. In every aspect of our lives, there will be frustrations and tensions. There will be seemingly unsurmountable problems to deal with. But that's life and it's all a part of being alive. I've said this before, and I'll say it again, the only people without problems are either six feet under or a pile of ashes in an urn. Part of life is learning to deal with all manner of frustrations, disappointments and challenges. If we accept them for what they are and look for all the positives in every situation, nothing will stop us from enjoying life.

Like the rain, every frustration, regret, disappointment and challenge, eventually comes to an end. The sun comes out and the world seems an even better place to live in. Our biggest challenge is not dealing with the challenges, it's accepting that they are part of life and embracing them. There isn't anything in life that isn't surmountable in one way or another. There is always a way out and always an alternative. The trick is to have the vision to see it.

The next time it's raining outside, I'm going to marvel at its life-giving properties, celebrate its sound, and thank my lucky stars I'm still here to appreciate its wonders.

Politics

We can't really get away from politics. In almost every situation imaginable, we find ourselves up against it. In the workplace, it's rampant, unless perhaps you're a sheep farmer on the Orkney Islands, but even then, you'd need to deal with other shepherds on the island and vie for your position. I have this theory that politics in the workplace is all about insecurity. If people aren't particularly good at their job, they become experts in politics. They spread rumours about those they feel threatened by and weave threads of deceit amongst gullible colleagues that are disingenuous and downright evil.

I loathe 'political' people because they are so insincere. They are particularly damaging for someone like me who wants to be open and honest about everything. They create a culture of suspicion that becomes truly toxic. They also manufacture an environment that forces talented, good and honest people out. They want an environment where mediocrity rules to make them feel more comfortable. It's the epitome of the tall poppy syndrome and it makes my blood boil. Why can't we celebrate everyone? Every one of us is different and every one of us has our own set of strengths. It's just a matter of identifying those strengths and putting them to good use. Why can't we celebrate the amazing talents amongst us and become their support team rather than an undermining influence? Work as a team to achieve the best we can in any given situation, not try to chop the heads off those we think are better than us. It's ludicrous.

Sadly, this is an uphill battle because of so much innate insecurity. Politics in the workplace is like bullying in the playground and is equally childish. It's as though some people never grow up. The playground gang is replaced by the workplace gang with similar ringleaders in charge. Each cohort is just as destructive and isolating. Of course, it's supposed to be the responsibility of management to stamp it out, but most just pay lip service to the idea of a bully-free environment because they themselves are controlled by the self-same bullies. Blah, blah, blah, blah goes the management's refrain whilst our brightest and finest continue to be chopped down to an acceptable size. The political bullies triumph once again and mediocrity rules. It's a sad, sad situation as Bernie and Elton put it.

It takes courage to ignore politics and not get entangled in those evil webs. It takes courage to celebrate talent in the face of underhand tactics, and it takes courage to stand up for what we believe in. But without courageous people in the world, nothing will change. It's never a matter of being defiant for the sake of bucking the trend, it's just a matter of being defiant when an injustice is taking place. We can't follow like sheep just because it's the easiest thing to do. We need to think for ourselves and not let political bullies make important decisions on our behalf. Condoning the destruction of immensely talented and good-natured people is bordering on criminality. I for one don't want to be part of it.

Reinvention

It's good to be back after a day off. I felt guilty about neglecting my diary, but sometimes life gets in the way. It shouldn't become a chore though, and I must be kind to myself. In fact, we should all be kind to ourselves and have the flexibility to be accepting.

I've had a good run of entries over the last few months with only the odd missed day. I've had highs and I've had lows, but on the whole, it's been a very positive experience. I think the trick is not to expect too much, too soon. Everything tends to go in waves. Waves of positivity and waves of negativity. As long as the waves don't turn into a tsunami, we should be content. Extremes in either direction are probably a sign of extremes in our nature, which might be cause for concern. Being level-headed is a good thing in these strange times. We really must be flexible when there is so much uncertainty around us. The world as a whole is in a state of flux, in just the same way that our individual lives can be in a state of flux. Adapt or cease to exist is a very Darwinian slant on it, but one well worth remembering.

I've found myself slipping back into old thinking habits recently and it's been very disappointing. I've found myself getting back on the failed relationship merry-go-round and I'm dizzy from it all. But to be honest, this isn't anything new and it's all part of those wave cycles. I have to see the bigger picture and realise that even though I might step back every now and then, on the whole, I'm still moving forward. As long as I realise what's happening and I'm accepting of the odd weakness, my recovery is still on track. These things take time and emotional damage is the hardest to recover from.

It really is a matter of constantly reminding ourselves that what has happened, has happened. No amount of reliving, or torturing ourselves is going to make the slightest bit of difference. The only thing we can do is gradually change our perception of events. By re-programming our minds into thinking that what transpired was for the best, will give us the freedom to reinvent ourselves. Reinventing ourselves, facilitates reinventing our lives. Once we discard the hurt, pain and betrayal, our new baggage-free world is full of possibilities. No matter what stage we're at in life, reinvention is possible. Every new day offers us another chance to start over. Every new day is full of potential and positivity if we only keep ourselves open to it.

I've been on this course for a long time now and it does work. I just need to keep doing it. Despite any setbacks, keep doing it. Keep reinventing yourself every day; keep reinventing yourself every moment of every precious day. The reinvention will be such a step up from the old model, life will be brilliant. Here's to today and the promise of tomorrow.

Words

Words can be a very powerful tool for changing our mindset. Just think of the number of times in our lives when a few well-chosen words of encouragement from someone else have transformed our mood. It's almost instantaneous joy and something to celebrate and savour. Words can be transformative when we hear them, but also when we use them.

If words are so powerful, we must be very careful with how we use them and how we receive them. We have the ability to help people through them or hinder people through them, so our goal should be to speak positively in every situation. Do we want to make a positive contribution to the world around us or a negative one? Well-chosen words will answer that question for sure.

In this diary about heartbreak, I've always tried to put a positive spin on things despite describing the immense pain that comes with the territory. We all experience pain in these situations and sometimes it seems almost impossible to deal with it. Our brains become filled with negative thoughts that revolve around grief, regret, resentment and betrayal—to name but a few—and it's an uphill battle trying to substitute words and feelings that balance these out. Grief, loss and regret must make way for new beginnings and a fresh start. Everything in life comes to an end at some point or renews itself and carries on in a different form. In its broadest sense, our life falls neatly into periods of change and transformation. We move from being a baby to a toddler and from a toddler to adolescence. From our adolescent years, we morph into teenagers and then young adults. Everything is gradual growth and change, adapting ourselves to the world around us. Sometimes, the changes are small and some of us retain a lifelong childish quality. Others are worn down by events and circumstances and become bitter and defensive. Childlike optimism remains for some and disappears for others.

The language we use has a big bearing on the state we assume. If we use upbeat and positive words, we have a better chance of living an upbeat and positive life. Transforming our vocabulary is therefore at the root of transforming our lives. Our brains are full of both sets of words and when we're down, the negative ones take charge. By replacing those with their positive opposites, we can facilitate an almost instantaneous change in our mood. By using positive words in our daily life, we will not only enhance the lives of the people around us, but also our own.

So yes, words are really powerful and we have them at our disposal to enhance the world. If we utilize their positive energy, every day will be a brighter day, no matter what's going on around us.

Staying True to Ourselves

I've had an amazing life really. I've travelled the world and fulfilled many professional goals. I also had a long and happy marriage until my wife called it quits and decided to move on to something different. I say different, because better implies that what we shared was not the real thing, and I think it was for a very long time. But that's all part of the heartbreak, learning to live with something that no longer exists.

Moving on is always going to be difficult for the person in the relationship who didn't think it was over. In fact, who never thought it could ever be over. It's a challenge I face every day of my life and it sometimes makes me feel very sad. For the last three months or so, I've been writing about this topic on a daily basis, trying my best to uncover any secret ways of dealing with this sadness. I've had some upbeat times when I've thought I'd cracked it and then there have been the usual times when the whole process has seemed a bit pointless. After analysing something so intently, there comes a point when we lose the wind in our sails and we just have to sit around and wait for things to improve.

I'm really grateful to the people who have supported my writing efforts, because writing about such personal things can be quite difficult. The self-doubt creeps in and you wonder if you have anything at all valuable to say. Getting positive reinforcement provides just that little confirmation that I'm not alone in the world grappling with these issues—other people are experiencing, or have experienced, the heartbreak too. I shouldn't be surprised of course, because heartbreak is an integral part of our culture. The number of songs that have been written about love and loss is legion. Every one of us will go through this experience at least once in our lives if not many more times. But it does seem to me that the deeper the emotional commitment was, the longer it takes to recover. My former wife was my first love and what a profound love it was too. Total commitment for 24 years. Utter devotion for 24 years. The pain is very real.

However, the last thing I want to do is sound like a love-forsaken, weak-willed man who is dying from a broken heart. What would that achieve? Nothing. By sharing my experiences, I'm hoping that we can all recover from this kind of painful experience and come out the other end intact and stronger. It doesn't really matter how we get there, as long as we get there. The danger occurs when we lose hope. We go around and around in circles and never find a way out. Constantly revisiting events in an attempt to find out what went wrong. Looking for that elusive thing that explains everything. Sadly, it doesn't seem to work like that. I've been doing this for the last three years and I still haven't stumbled on that elusive 'thing' that explains everything.

But we don't need to find anything to explain everything. We don't need a 'thing' to have hope. What provides hope is the fact that we are good, loyal human beings who loved with the kind of intensity only dreams are made of. Despite whatever happened, that was our legacy, that was our strength and that was our point of difference. And that is who we are. As long as we stay true to ourselves, there will always be hope. Fortunately, the world is full of people like us. People who have integrity, honesty and loyalty. We have nothing to be ashamed of, we have plenty of things to celebrate. Let the betrayers continue to live their sordid lives. Our pain comes from who we are as people, their lack of it comes from who they are as people. I'm happy to deal with the pain, thanks.

Let's Not Be Eaten for Lunch

'The time has come, the Walrus said, to talk of many things.' This line from Lewis Carroll's poem The Walrus and the Carpenter sums everything up. It is time to talk of many things, because sharing ideas at every level is what makes the world go round. It's also a great way of getting things off our minds and clearing them of unnecessary clutter.

When I woke up this morning, my mind was buzzing with negative thoughts of pointlessness. It's a funny phrase that: negative thoughts of pointlessness. But I think it sums up a state of negative brain freeze, where no matter what you think, it leads you back to unhelpful areas you'd rather avoid. We all go through it at one time or another, but when it starts to get ingrained, we need to rally our blocking techniques and reboot the brain programming channels. These states creep up on us so subtly, they take hold before we even know about it. One random negative thought leads to another. It really is the scourge of the world and a hidden scourge at that. As I contemplated my negative thoughts of pointlessness, I was fully aware of the futility of this mental activity. Why am I letting my brain become filled with negativity when it could be filled with positivity? Why do we allow this mental virus to take hold of our most precious organ? What is it about human nature that actually encourages 'accentuating the negative and eliminating the positive' rather than following the original song lyric?

I think the traumas we experience in life make us more susceptible to this kind of thinking. If we hit rock bottom enough times, we are programmed for the journey. In a way, because of repetition, the journey is safe and weirdly comforting. That is, until we get to the destination, which is anything but safe and comforting. We toss thoughts of the past around in our brains and wallow in their feel-goodness. We know where it's going to lead, but we can't help ourselves. Soon, the outside world has no influence and all the good things that are going on around us are invisible. Our brain becomes a cauldron of negative thoughts and we don't seem to have an escape route.

But we do, we really do have an escape route. We need to view all these thoughts objectively and understand that they are only thoughts. There is nothing tangible about them and they were created by us and no one else. We have *chosen* to perpetuate the thought patterns; we have *chosen* to allow these negative thoughts to take control of our brains. They have not been injected from an external source, they exist and will only grow if we feed them. Our task is to replace every negative thought with a positive one. The outside world doesn't give a damn if we are walking around with a pile of negative thoughts in our heads or a pile of positive ones. Admittedly, with positive thoughts in our heads, we will undoubtedly have much more meaningful interactions with other people. But ultimately, the only people we are harming are ourselves.

I know I've been down this road before (and maybe I'll go down it again) but each time I do, I realise how pointless it is. I realise that it's within my power to change things if I only make a big enough effort. What has happened to us in the past has no bearing on our now or our future. We either choose to be positive, upbeat and truly alive, or we choose to be negative, downbeat and one of the walking dead.

If we are gullible enough to give in to those persuasive negative thoughts, we'll end up like the oysters in The Walrus and the Carpenter, and be eaten for lunch.

Moving Day

Today is the day before moving day for me. We are going to a bigger property by the beach, so will enjoy some amazing sunsets. It also means I'll be able to see what the tide is doing and walk the beach every day. Beach walking therapy has become a way of life for me in recent years and it's the ideal way to deal with a whole host of mental baggage.

These little written vignettes have moved their focus from heartbreak to broader issues of keeping happy and I'm pleased about that. The heartbreak cycle can become very tiresome and once you've explored every imaginable facet, repetition becomes the norm. I end up going around and around in circles and reaching the only conclusion I can: we need to move on and time is the eventual healer. But after a rough time, our spirits often take a bashing and it's difficult to be energised by anything. Even a move to the beach doesn't have the same excitement it once would have held.

That's where trying to improve our overall mental health comes into play. We need to savour the small things in life and celebrate every aspect of it. Even packing can go from being a chore to something of an adventure. Providing we haven't forced ourselves into a situation where everything is last minute, we can plan the stages step by step and enjoy the process. Yes, change in itself can be a bit daunting, but without change, there is no room for renewal, and without renewal, stagnation sets in. It's important to remember that everything starts from within. Our thought processes are what keep us healthy. Toxic thought processes lead to toxic conditions in every aspect of our lives. The simplest of activities can become insurmountable hurdles with toxic thinking. The most complicated tasks can be overcome with ease with an open mind and a logical approach. The contrasts can be immense.

When we free ourselves from toxic thinking, everything in life becomes easy. Everyday challenges are a breeze and everyday annoyances dissipate before our eyes or don't even register. Our interactions with other people progress to another level, because they can sense that we are at ease with ourselves. We project optimism and hope, not doom and gloom. We become glass-half-full people with a positive slant on everything. People don't want to be in a toxic atmosphere, they want to be in a positive, 'nothing is impossible' mindset that can overcome anything. There are countless stories of people who have hit rock bottom but have then managed to transform their lives into something amazing and purposeful. Anthony Robbins, the self-help guru, is one example and there are literally hundreds in that field. Their purpose in life became helping other people. Their mission became a burning desire to help people help themselves. To teach people how to overcome their own inner demons and move forwards. The cynical side of us may well scoff at their transformational theories and obvious money-making abilities, but at least they are making the effort and whether we like it or not, they are changing a lot of lives.

Transformation really does come from within, and if I've learnt anything in the last few years, it's that. External influences reflect what has already happened within us, they are not what causes what has happened within us. Just think of the moments in your life when everything seemed to be going swimmingly. Your spirits were up, your confidence high and you appeared unstoppable. Ninety per cent of this came from within and the world reflected it back again. The point is, whether the world *actually* reflected this positivity back again is immaterial, you were on a roll and unstoppable.

We can be like this every day of our lives if we decide to train our brains to think in a certain way. You can't become physically fit without consistent training and you certainly can't become mentally fit without the same rigorous preparation. I'm determined to use my beach walks for both purposes.

A Dog's Life

Good morning, world! It's been quite a while since I made a diary entry and I've been missing my writing time. It's been a busy period moving house and settling into a new area. It wasn't a massive move, but enough to upset my daily routines. Without consistency, it's difficult to achieve anything worthwhile. But sometimes, life sets us some challenges and all we can do is be pragmatic and take up from where we left off whenever we can.

I mustn't complain though, the new house is right on a beautiful beach and I wake up to stunning views and go to bed looking at an incredible sunset. My surroundings are idyllic and I'm very lucky in so many ways. I think I was also getting to a point with my diary where my internal struggles were becoming repetitive. After four months of daily heartbreak analysis, I'd bled the subject dry. I'd actually achieved what I wanted to achieve: an acceptance that life must go on and an understanding that I just need to learn to live with what happened. Reading through many of my past entries, I realise that it's been a very important journey for me. I've managed to take the sting out of my heartbreak's tail. It's always going to be there, but it's not going to rule my life. Having said that, I still find my thoughts returning to all that happened on a daily basis and there remains an inner sadness that's hard to describe.

Maybe the new, post-heartbreak me, is just a me with a tinge of sadness added. The picture is the same, but the hues are paler. I'm a bit washed out by the whole experience and maybe only time will bring back my true colour. But maybe not? Maybe I'll just have to live with the sadness and that will be a new part of my character. Every one of life's experiences moulds us into who we are. When the experiences are good, we assume an air of optimism and hope, when they're bad, we have an air of melancholy that's hard to quantify. But we are all made up of these components and we simply must choose to get the balance right. Constant dwelling in the past gives us a sad demeanour. Too much optimism can create a shallow, flippant person, who seems unable to face up to what has happened to them. We need to mix our palette of colours wisely or our portrait will be a mess.

I've just been watching a couple of regulars on the beach. A noisy dog and his owner. The dog just can't get enough of the ball the owner throws into the sea for him to retrieve. He barks after delivering the ball and wants more and more. He has an insatiable desire to retrieve. Other dogs do the same thing, but quietly, this dog wants the world to know how important this ritual is. It just goes to show that we're all different and we all have different ways of presenting ourselves to the world. Some of us wish to share our personal experiences with the world, while others are content to deal with everything that comes our way secretly. Some of us may be intensely private people, but also have a burning desire to make the world a better place; to share our own experiences in an effort to help other people get through the same challenges. To expose our own weaknesses in an effort to debunk the idea that weakness is a bad thing. When we are in immense emotional pain, it helps to know we're not the only ones experiencing such trauma. It helps to know that there are other people out there experiencing the same challenges and working through the same thought processes. It helps to know that other people have been equally mucked up by relationship turmoil.

Having read back through so many of my old entries, I realised that three of them came with the title 'Acceptance.' Acceptance is such an important part of living a happy life. Without it, we can't possibly move forward. But it's also important we don't confuse acceptance with capitulation. Acceptance of things beyond our control is one thing, acceptance of something we can change for the better is another. I might have accepted a certain part of me died in the course of my heartbreak, but I need to have the conviction that what died will be replaced by an unimaginably more powerful rebirth. An understanding that life is richer because of my experiences and in spite of my experiences. I get to watch the ocean, and the dog's life I experienced today, is a hell of a lot better than the dog's life I lived before.

Chewing the Cud

I often wonder if the world around me is real. Am I just making it all up and creating an illusionary life populated by people from my imagination? It's an interesting thought. That would be a real case of being master of my own destiny. I'm sure philosophers through the ages have grappled with such ideas in an attempt to make sense of who they are and what they're doing on the planet. To some extent, what we experience is always illusionary since we rely on so much information that comes from secondary sources. In past centuries, people thought the world was flat and if you sailed far enough towards the horizon, you'd eventually drop off the end. They truly believed that, so that was as real to them as us knowing the world is round and accepting that we stay on it because of gravity. But most of us only know this from second-hand information. So much of what we experience in life is based on information we can't actually confirm.

Many of us go through life from cradle to grave following structures that have been created for us. Believing in things that have been presented to us as the truth, and not questioning anything that could rock the boat of these perceptions. Conformity keeps order and allows society to function. But it also creates robots with little imagination and little sense of discovery. Every one of us on the planet has an incredible brain capable of infinite thinking power and yet only a fraction of us use just a small part of our brain's potential. A small number of the population think for the rest of the population. Likewise, a fraction of the population becomes custodians of the world's wealth. Thinking on a large scale is therefore dangerous for those chosen few since it steals their rarity value.

So, life is a bit of an illusion if we don't challenge what we perceive. If we don't question what we're fed, we'll live a life that other people have created for us. We'll be like animals raised to be eaten. Chewing our way through the cud of life with no idea of our impending doom. Collective consciousness could be put to much better use. Harnessing the brain power of the whole population through education could reap infinite resources that could actually save us as a species. Instead of dumbing everyone down, society should be building everyone up. Instead of two per cent of the population being in charge of ninety per cent of the wealth, everything should be spread evenly. Good education should be available to everyone, so that we are tapping all the potential of this tiny planet spinning in the middle of nowhere. But maybe the world is flat after all and we doubters, will get in a boat, head for the horizon and just fall off the end.

I think the moral of today's story is that whatever we do in life is dependent on what we choose to perceive. We have a brain capable of weighing up the evidence and making informed decisions. Our ability to think and reason gives us choices. And as this diary is about failed relationships, we have the ability to recover from an emotional trauma if we wish to. The choice is ours alone. How we choose to perceive the situation is entirely our prerogative. In this instance, society is not dictating our fate, we are. Society doesn't give a damn about our heartbreak and as a general rule, society doesn't give a damn about our mental health. It just wants us to shut up, chew the cud and wait for the inevitable end. Let's jump the fence, do away with the herd instinct and make our life what we want it to be, not what someone else wants it to be.

Don't Look Up

Over the last few days, I've watched the film *Don't Look Up* and whilst it's obviously meant to be something of a black comedy, it's also a scary representation of the fickle nature of the society we live in today. People can be coerced into thinking whatever the politicians want them to think. A huge chunk of rock can be heading straight towards the earth with doom written all over it and yet denial can prevail. It's the ultimate example of a collective heads-in-the-sand mentality. I'm not really sure what the answer is and I'm not sure the filmmakers knew either. The perpetrators of this mass denial are the only ones who survive the ultimate impact, jetting off into space and finding a host planet that will support life even better than Earth. The irony is that when they emerge from their 22,000-odd years of induced hibernation, they get their heads bitten off by a Pterodactyl lookalike—I guess it's some kind of divine retribution!

Talking of Pterodactyls, I dreamt about my ex again last night. It's an amusing segue, but it belies the grief I felt. Even after nearly three years, I'm still emotionally fragile. She was being her usual aloof self and I was crying. I've done a lot of crying in the last three years and there seems no end to it. The crying has almost ceased in my waking moments—although my heart still bleeds—but the tears still roll in my dreams. I guess a love as intense as the one I had for my ex takes some time to fade. I just wonder if it will ever let me go. No doubt as she did the dirty on me, she has moved on remarkably well and is enjoying a blessed new life devoid of any feelings of regret. The coldness in her approach to ending our relationship of 24 years has presumably continued; the ends presumably justified the means in her mind. But denial is a tricky business and once the newness of the newness wears off, maybe such people always end up getting their heads bitten off. In a way, I hope for divine retribution, but in another way, the love I still feel prevents me from wanting it to happen. The love is now illusionary of course, as it's just based on memories of the person I first married, not the woman she became.

I think the kind of love I experienced is rare in this ever-so-fake world. It really was 'from the bottom of my heart' stuff. I still experience it vividly in my dreams. I can still feel it in my bones. Maybe death will be my only final release? Be that as it may, I need to find a way of living with it. I need to find a way of coping with this never-ending heartbreak. I don't want the rest of my life to be tinged with such sadness. I want my heart and my eyes to stop bleeding. I want this immense weight of grief to be lifted so that I can soar like a bird and chase a stick like a dog. I want to be free to love again with the same intensity, devoid of guilt. I just wish the love I felt for my ex would let me go. The trouble is, I never betrayed it, she did. Old habits die hard, but I can't hold onto something that no longer exists.

Looking out over the sea now that the sun has come up, fills me with hope. Every day is a new day in this great journey through life. My troubles are small compared to a possible end to the world. Fortunately, something like that isn't on the cards at this moment in time, so we should all make the most of what we have and celebrate life. I'll just have to continue searching for my own inner peace, but enjoy life as best I can. I hope you will do the same.

Printed in the USA
CPSIA information can be obtained
at www.ICGtesting.com
LVHW080059031223
765141LV00065B/1036

9 781398 498471